LOUCA-MAI BRADY
BERNI GRAHAM

SOCIAL RESEARCH WITH CHILDREN AND YOUNG PEOPLE

A practical guide

POLICY PRESS SHORTS POLICY & PRACTICE

First published in Great Britain in 2019 by

Policy Press
University of Bristol
1-9 Old Park Hill
Bristol
BS2 8BB
UK
t: +44 (0)117 954 5940
pp-info@bristol.ac.uk
www.policypress.co.uk

North America office:
Policy Press
c/o The University of Chicago Press
1427 East 60th Street
Chicago, IL 60637, USA
t: +1 773 702 7700
f: +1 773 702 9756
sales@press.uchicago.edu
www.press.uchicago.edu

British Library Cataloguing in Publication Data
A catalogue record for this book is available from the British Library.

Library of Congress Cataloging-in-Publication Data
A catalog record for this book has been requested.

ISBN 978-1-4473-5114-6 (paperback)
ISBN 978-1-4473-5115-3 (ePub)
ISBN 978-1-4473-5116-0 (Mobi)

Cover design by Policy Press
Front cover: image kindly supplied by Shutterstock
Printed and bound in Great Britain by CMP, Poole
Policy Press uses environmentally responsible print partners

Contents

List of illustrations

Notes on authors

Dr Louca-Mai Brady is a Research Associate at Kingston University and St George's Joint Faculty of Health, Social Care and Education and an independent research consultant. She has had a long career in research with children and young people and her research interests include health and social care, disability and participative research methods. Louca-Mai's research career to date has focused on social research which has practical applications for policy and practice. She is interested in research as a tool for social change, both through undertaking research which has direct relevance to children and young people's lived experience and using participatory approaches to support children's and young people's involvement in the research process. Her work has included research and evaluation projects both about and with diverse groups of children and young people, including young disabled people, young people with experience of substance misuse treatment and those affected by adverse childhood experiences.

In 2017 she was awarded a PhD for a participative research study on 'embedding children and young people's participation in health services and research', in which young people were involved as young advisers and in co-production workshops alongside health professionals. As a researcher, consultant and trainer Louca-Mai seeks to put children and young people's experiences, and children's rights, at the heart of research.

Berni Graham is an independent senior researcher, with 18 years' experience of research and evaluation, specialising in issues affecting children and young people and their families. This follows a lengthy career in social policy and health. Berni is particularly interested in capturing the voices of those least often heard, and helping these to be reflected in policy, practice and service delivery. She has worked with diverse groups from all backgrounds. Berni designs and conducts research and evaluations for a range of UK agencies, including the Department of Education, Contact, Mencap, National Children's Bureau (NCB), Mind, Prince's Trust, Sure Start and Ipsos-Mori, and covers a variety of subjects, including physical and mental health, learning and physical disability, poverty, young carers, looked after children, education, early years and special needs. She often adopts a mixed methodology, including qualitative, quantitative and creative methods and evidence reviews to help ensure all perspectives are explored. She regularly gets asked to advise and support other agencies on method and tool design.

Along with Louca-Mai, Berni co-designs and delivers several courses a year for the Social Research Association (SRA), training researchers on doing research with children and young people and public involvement. She previously designed and delivered training for the NCB, Princes Trust and other agencies. She has also trained several groups of young people as peer researchers, including a group of care leavers.

She is a co-writer of the SRA revised ethical guidelines (due in 2019).

1
INTRODUCTION

There is increasing interest in children's and young people's participation in research, both as direct sources of data and through their active involvement in, and input into, research design and processes. The book is designed to be of practical assistance to researchers undertaking social research and evaluation with children and young people. It also provides research users (for example policy makers and practitioners), commissioners and others with an understanding of the key issues to consider when using or commissioning social research and evaluation with children and young people. It provides an overview of the theoretical and UK legal and policy context, and provides a practical overview of key ethical, methodological and other considerations, including the use of creative, inclusive and participative research approaches

In developing and writing this book we have drawn on our own extensive practical experience of social research and evaluation with a wide variety of children and young people, using a range of methods and methodologies. We also draw on the questions and issues raised by participants on the training courses we have been running for the Social Research Association for several years, particularly calls for clear, practical guidance. The book therefore includes examples and checklists to aid readers in understanding how to apply the points in this book to their own research and evaluation studies. While it is intended to be an introductory overview, this book provides extensive links to further reading and other sources of information.

As well as ensuring that children and young people generally get a voice, we both have a particular interest in capturing the realities and perceptions of more vulnerable and marginalised children and young people. This includes disabled children and young people, those growing up in poverty, those affected by adverse childhood experiences and others who are disadvantaged, 'socially excluded' and/or have additional needs. Therefore, this book has a focus on making research and evaluation with children and young people as inclusive, accessible and wide-reaching as possible in its coverage of recruitment, ethical issues, designing appropriate methods and tools, reporting and dissemination.

We also have a keen interest in, and extensive experience of, promoting and supporting the involvement of children and young people in all stages of the research process. The book therefore explores both children and young people as research subjects (as a source of data) and their involvement in the research process.

This introductory chapter sets the scene and outlines:

- the case for research with children and young people
- what we mean by 'children and young people'
- the scope of this book

Why do research with children and young people?

In traditional research methodologies, the perspectives of children and young people were often filtered through the interpretations of adults, both parents and carers, as 'proxies' for children and young people, and by adult researchers. But children and young people are citizens, with agency and lived experience as well as a right, under the United Nations (UN) Convention on the Rights of the Child, to have a say in matters which affect them.

Doing research and evaluation directly with children and young people, and/or involving them in the research process, helps to improve the research depth and richness as discussed further in Chapters Three to Five.

Benefits to research and services

- Getting views, opinions and insights directly from children and young people can lead to better research.
- Children and young people, who are the ultimate end users of policy programmes and services, can provide input to help shape and improve these for their peers.
- Getting children's and young people's direct input can help reflect their lived realities, experiences and priorities in policy and service design.

Benefits to children and young people

- Most children and young people, like adults, enjoy giving their views about their lived experience and exercising their right to have a say in matters that affect them.
- Having their views and opinions respected by adults, and seeing how this can lead to positive change, may encourage some to be more confident about using their right to a voice.
- Research participants and/or their peers may benefit from any improvements made to policy or services.
- Being involved in research, as a participant or through improvement in the research process, can help children and young people to gain new knowledge, experience and skills.

Key challenges when doing research with children and young people

Assumptions about children's and young people's ability, insight, maturity or understanding: It is not uncommon for researchers, those who work with children and parents or carers to presume that a child or young person would be unable to make a useful contribution to research, or that their need for protection overrides their right to participate.

Ensuring diversity in sampling: Children and young people are far from homogeneous. Gathering only the views or experiences of the 'easiest to reach' can lead to research which is unrepresentative and may, for example, exclude the views of those most likely to use services. Inclusive research with children and young people can take time and effort and require additional resources.

Insufficient planning: Various aspects of the research process usually need additional time and planning when doing research or evaluation with children and young people. For example, when sampling and recruiting, agreement is needed from professionals, parents or carers, who also need sufficient information. If the research needs ethical clearance, research ethics committees often require additional processes and reassurances for research with children and young people. Children and young people may not have prior experience of research and the consent process, and data collection may require more time than with adults. Research tools also need careful consideration, designing appropriate and accessible methods for different ages and abilities can take some time and work best if tried and tested with the target group.

There are *additional dimensions to ethical issues* when doing research with children and young people, not least around informed consent and confidentiality.

Defining 'children and young people'

Age definitions

Childhood has many and varied definitions including 'the status of being a minor, the early-life state of immaturity whether actual or ascribed and the process of growing towards adulthood' (Alderson, 2013, p 4). Legislatively, in relation to most education and children's services, 'children' are generally understood to be those from birth up to the age of 18, (McNeish, 1999). However, both legally and in many policy contexts, the upper-age limit varies. For instance, disabled children, those with special educational needs and some looked after children (children in public care) are often entitled to support until the age of 25. Meanwhile, 'youth' or 'young people' are commonly defined as those aged 15–25 in terms of service delivery but can occasionally include those aged up to 35 (UNESCO, 2016).

This book focuses on gathering data directly from children and young people, in other words rather than from, or as well as from, parents, carers or professionals. Chapters Four and Five cover the need to design or adapt approaches and materials according to a child's or young person's cognitive ability, rather than strictly by physical age. In practice most researchers are likely to work with children of school age (4 and over) and young people up to different ages (according to circumstances, issues, or services being used). However, we also include information and further resources on conducting research with very young children.

Encompassing the diversity of children and young people

Although 'children and young people' is a widely used term, they are far from being a homogeneous group. When planning appropriate research, researchers need to consider all children and young people and their diversity, particularly when determining how to design sampling and methodology. Apart from age, this 'group' varies immensely by ethnicity, culture, disability, gender, socioeconomic situation, living circumstances and other factors. Put another way, when conducting a study of adults, age would not be only categorisation used. Children and young people live in a wide variety of communities and family and other circumstances, with associated variation in social exclusion and access to services and opportunities. In Chapters Three to Five we discuss how to take an inclusive approach, which necessitates looking beyond the easiest to reach and the most frequently heard. But we also explore the need for balance, being aware of the risk of over-researching some sub-groups and children's and young people's right not to be involved.

Book structure

Chapters Two to Five cover a range of theoretical and practical issues that need to be considered by those planning social research and evaluation with children and young people. Each chapter includes practical tips and guidance and references for further reading.

Chapter Two explores the context for the growing interest in research with children and young people. The chapter summarises how discourses around children's rights, changing views of the nature of childhood and ideas about children's agency and citizenship inform approaches to research with children and young people. We consider how this theoretical context is reflected in UK legislation and policy, and the implications of this for social research and evaluation.

Chapter Three makes the case for involving children and young people in the research process and their working alongside researchers in the design and delivery of research (children and young people as research participants are explored in Chapters Four and Five). The chapter outlines both the theory and practice of children's and young people's involvement, the different forms involvement can take, and provides practical guidance on how to ensure that involvement is meaningful, realisable, effective and inclusive.

Chapter Four covers the ethical considerations required when doing social research and evaluation with children and young people and ways to address any issues. For example, it looks at the balance required between maximising participation and creating benefit, while protecting children and young people from harm. It covers the extra considerations around sampling, working with gatekeepers, informed consent, minimising bias, ensuring confidentiality, privacy and anonymity, and particular dimensions when using different methods.

Chapter Five sets out key considerations in designing robust methods and tools to suit diverse groups of children and young people, while minimising any potential negative impact from taking part in research or evaluation. We explore the considerations needed to make topics, concepts, language and tools both accessible and appealing for different ages, needs and abilities, how to design more 'creative methods' and ways to approach covering sensitive topics and research with younger participants.

Chapter Six summarises the key considerations highlighted in the previous chapters. The Bibliography provides further information and guidance.

References

Alderson, P. (2013) *Childhoods Real and Imagined, vol 1: An Introduction to Critical Realism and Childhood Studies.* London: Routledge.

McNeish, D. (1999) Promoting participation for children and young people: some key questions for health and social welfare organisations. *Journal of Social Work Practice: Psychotherapeutic Approaches in Health, Welfare and the Community*, 13(2): 191–203.

UNESCO (2016) What do we mean by youth? Available from: www. unesco.org/new/en/social-and-human-sciences/themes/youth/ youth-definition/

2
THE CONTEXT FOR SOCIAL RESEARCH WITH CHILDREN AND YOUNG PEOPLE

Introduction

A focus on children's rights and changing views around the nature of childhood has, to some extent, been reflected in a growing interest in children's and young people's participation in research. This includes both research on children and young people (as sources of data) and their active involvement in the research process. In the chapters that follow, we explore the methodological and ethical questions that arise in relation to social research and evaluation with children and young people, but first we need to consider the epistemological questions which underpin this research. This chapter provides an overview of the theoretical context to research with children and young people. It sets out why research should be carried out in ways that enable children and young people, as opposed to their parents, professionals or service providers, to be listened to. We argue that recognising that children and young people are experts in their own lives is vital to ensuring that research, evaluation and the policies and services which they inform, better reflect children's and young people's priorities and concerns. The chapter explores:

- children's rights;
- key theory, including childhood studies and ideas of children's agency and citizenship;
- the legislative and policy context for research with children and young people.

Children's rights

The growth of sociological interest in children and young people has coincided broadly with the development of the modern children's rights movement (Mayall, 2015; Qvortrup et al, 2009). Children's rights are underpinned by the United Nations (UN) Convention on the Rights of the Child (CRC; UN, 1989), which encompasses social, economic, civil and political rights. The CRC is the most widely ratified human rights treaty in the world, accepted by all UN member states except the United States, and came into force in the UK in 1992. It sets out children's rights in terms of both their protection and their participation in society and 'asserts children's right to have a voice in decision-making, as well as rights to freedom of thought and expression' (Percy-Smith and Thomas, 2010, p 1). Article 12, the key article relating to participation, states that:

> States Parties shall assure to the child who is capable of forming his or her own views the right to express those views freely in all matters affecting the child, the views of the child being given due weight in accordance with the age and maturity of the child. (UN, 1989, Article 12)

The CRC-informed understanding that children and young people should be involved in decisions which affect them is increasingly reflected in law, regulation, policy and research guidance. Further, Article 13 states that children have the right to seek, receive and impart information and ideas of all kinds. The realisation of children's participation rights requires their translation into policy and practice;

as well as children's and young people's participation in conceptualising and realising these rights (Spronk, 2014).

Children's rights are about more than children's and young people's right to have a say in matters that affect them; the CRC recognises that children and young people 'also have particular needs and vulnerabilities that require special protection beyond the rights to which adults are entitled' (Groundwater-Smith et al, 2015, p 6). The CRC also sets out the responsibilities of adults to provide guidance to children and young people and to protect them from harm (McNeish, 1999). Participation rights do not operate in a vacuum and in planning research with children and young people it is important to also consider their welfare and protection rights:

> While the UNCRC does assign some autonomy rights, these are framed by an overarching concern with 'the best interests of the child', those interests not being treated as identical with a child's desires or preferences ... Furthermore, the autonomy rights that the UNCRC grants are explicitly constrained by judgments on the part of adults as regards the competence of the children concerned. (Hammersley, 2015, p 572)

Both parents and professionals often 'take a protective stance towards children to act in their best interest' (Coyne and Harder, 2011, p 12). This links back to the idea of competence discussed in relation to children's participation rights above: adults' views of whether children and young people are able to participate in research will be determined by their own views on competence, understanding and maturity. If children and young people are felt to be particularly vulnerable, that participation might be seen as potentially disruptive to their well-being (Vis et al, 2011). In other words, gatekeepers may decide that they will not assist with recruitment or support a child or young person's participation in a research study if they have concerns that taking part will have potential negative implications. This could lead to tension between participation and protection rights. Furthermore:

r-emphasising and even imposing a perceived vulnerability and needy dependence on [children and young people] ... while underestimating their competencies and freedom rights ... can increase their vulnerability and social exclusion and reduce their means to resist oppressive power. (Alderson, 2013, p 10)

How children's rights are interpreted and enabled often depends on adults' views of their competence, 'best interests' and how they conceptualise childhood and youth.

Understanding 'childhood'

'Childhood' is a social construction and how we conceptualise children and young people influences practices and approaches towards working with them (Tisdall et al, 2014). That is not to say that research with adults about children's and young people's lives is not valid and important, but that this should be as well as – not instead of – research with children and young people. Theoretical approaches to childhood in Western societies (the focus of this book) have in the past been dominated by paternalistic ideas of children and young people as needy, incompetent and vulnerable (Moss and Petrie, 2002). Developmental psychology suggests 'that what children mainly do during childhood is develop towards adulthood [and the] ... basic idea of developmentalism permeates policy-making and practice' (Mayall, 2015, p 79). This is particularly evident in the idea that children and young people are above all to be protected and provided for in order that they may develop well and be prepared to enter the public domain upon reaching adulthood (Mayall, 2015). In traditional research methodologies the perspectives of children and young people are often filtered through the interpretations of adults, both parents and carers as 'proxies' for children and young people, and by adult researchers. Researching children's and young people's lives through the views and understandings of the adults in their lives positions the child as an object rather than a subject of research and excludes their voice(s) from the research process (Christensen and James, 2008).

In considering why, how and when to do social research and evaluation with children and young people it is of course important to do so in ways which are ethical and appropriate. However, as discussed in the previous section on 'Children's rights', in seeking to protect children and young people we must ensure we do not deny them the opportunity to participate in research. There are tensions between 'researchers who seek to empower children to participate and hear their opinions and those who seek to regulate studies to protect children and their right to privacy' (Richards et al, 2015, p 3). While it is important for researchers to be sensitive to these issues 'an approach that regards the two as complementary rather than oppositional' (Richards et al, 2015, p 4) is important in order to enable children and young people to be active participants in research. The chapters that follow explore how to do this in as inclusive a way as possible.

Childhood studies

Childhood studies, and in particular sociology of childhood, focuses on children as well as childhood and challenges traditional developmental ideas of children and young people as 'becomings' rather than 'beings' (Qvortrup et al, 2009). This approach developed paradigms of children and young people as social actors and childhood as a social space in which children and young people can and do have agency and are experts in their own lives (Mayall, 2015):

Childhood studies ... pays close attention to children's issues, experiences and rights and to methods suited to exploring and identifying children's rights. (Smith and Greene, 2014, p 2)

Children and young people are seen as competent to share their views and opinions (James and Prout, 1997) but also constantly changing and evolving (Lansdown, 2006). In childhood studies:

children are recognised as social agents who share in shaping their own lives and influencing the world around them ... [they]

are respected as reliable research participants and sometimes co-researchers with their own valuable views and experiences. (Alderson, 2013, p 34)

This approach shifts the focus from research in which children were often in the margins, subsumed into research on families and households, rather than as objects of interest in their own right (Smith and Greene, 2014). Childhood studies have informed policy, practice and research agendas which incorporate the traditional protection of children and young people with an awareness of their rights to participation (Tisdall, 2012). They also provide the epistemological underpinnings of this book. A rights-based approach 'shifts the construct of children from individuals having needs to persons with entitlements to have their needs met', by acknowledging that they are the 'subjects of rights ... with the capacity to influence matters of concern to them' (Lansdown et al, 2016, p 253).

However, one of the challenges of taking a rights-based approach to children's and young people's participation in research is that competence, maturity and understanding are subjective and develop over time (Hart, 2008). Parents and professionals do of course have duties to protect and provide developmental opportunities for the children and young people for whom they are responsible. The challenge for children's and young people's participation is when adults impose their own perspectives, consciously or unconsciously, on children, or have different perspectives on what is in a child's or young person's best interests (Ehrich et al, 2015). If the child's views are seen as less important, or less valid, than adults' views, this will influence if and how they are involved in research. Therefore it is important to consider how best to engage with 'gatekeepers' (see the previous section, 'Children's rights'), as well as your own practices and approaches as a researcher. When doing research with children and young people you should consider 'the beliefs and assumptions researchers hold in relation to children, including their competence, rights and role within the research' (Dockett et al, 2011, p 69). Different levels of support which may be necessary for children and young people to give fully informed consent, and different methods will be appropriate for different children and young people in different circumstances, as discussed further in subsequent chapters. Chapter Three explores further how children and young people can be involved in the research process.

Children's agency and citizenship

Sociology of childhood, as already discussed in the section on 'Childhood studies', draws our attention to the positioning of children and young people in society relative to adults, their citizenship status and their capacity to participate fully as members of society (Cockburn, 1998; Devine, 2002). Lister (2007, p 694) argues that 'the language of citizenship has a contribution to make over and above that of [children's] rights'. Citizenship can be constructed as both an expression of human agency and as a right enabling children and young people to act as agents, rather than a legal status alone (Lister, 2007). As well as emphasising individual rights, considering research with children and young people through the lens of citizenship highlights the collective agency of children and young people through recognition of common issues (Dockett et al, 2011), and activity 'characterised by agency on the part of young people, as well as collective action towards social change' (Shaw et al, 2014). Despite their marginalisation within society, children and young people: 'are in reality already participating de facto as active citizens within the spaces of their everday lifeworlds' (Percy-Smith, 2016, p 403).

Such 'informal active citizenship' provides an alternative to 'adult decision-making according to the agenda, priorities and initiatives of adult professionals', in which children and young people are able to participate 'in spaces of their choosing and in ways they decide ... as active citizens' (Percy-Smith, 2016, p 413). In other words, seeing them as citizens, who have rights, agency and are experts in their own lives is central to meaningful and effective research both on and with children and young people.

Child voice in UK legislation and policy

The understanding that children and young people should be involved in decisions which affect them has been reflected increasingly in UK legislation and policy, including the Children Act 1989 and 2004, Children (Scotland) Act 1995, Children (Northern Ireland) Order 1995, Every Child Matters (Department for Education and Skills) 2003, and the Children and Families Act 2014. Public involvement is a key element of the Health and Social Care Act 2012. These policies 'were designed primarily to assert and protect the interests and rights of children' but also promote 'child voice by implying that children should be encouraged to contribute to decisions that affect them' (Richards et al, 2015, p 3). For example, the annual report by the Chief Medical Officer for England talked about the expectation inherent in the National Health Service Constitution:

> that patients, service users and the public participate nationally and locally in the development, implementation and accountability processes of health and social care policy and services … This expectation for patient and public participation has no age limit. Children and young people … should be encouraged and facilitated to participate in decisions about their own care and, more broadly, about the health and social care services and policies that affect them. (Department of Health, 2013, chapter 4, p 2)

Rhetoric and reality

However, while the language of children's rights has been widely employed in legislation and policy as outlined above, there is a lack of evidence for whether and how these rights are enabled in practice, and whether this has necessarily always led to improved outcomes for children and young people (Ferguson, 2013), or on policy making and service delivery (Byrne and Lundy, 2015; Crowley, 2015). State parties who have signed the CRC are required to report to the UN

Committee on the Rights of the Child (UNCRC) every five years on the steps they have taken to implement the articles of the convention.

The Children's Rights Alliance for England (CRAE) report on UK implementation of the CRC (CRAE, 2015) argues that the government report to the UN (HM Government, 2014) failed to fully address the recommendations previously made by the UN Committee on the Rights of the Child (UNCRC, 2009). These recommendations aimed to ensure that all children and young people have all their rights respected with enforceable means of redress. While acknowledging that some aspects of the CRC had been replicated in UK legislation, the CRAE (2015) report criticises the failure of successive UK governments to take forward the UN Committee's recommendation to expressly incorporate the CRC into domestic law, or as a statutory obligation in relation to the development of policy which affects children and young people. They suggest that this has resulted in a piecemeal approach, which means that rights are dependent on where children and young people are located or what services they receive, rather than being the entitlement of every child without discrimination (CRAE, 2015). The target-driven cultures of public sector providers can also undermine attempts at participation through barriers such as inflexible bureaucratic structures, which may be at odds with the priorities and concerns of children and young people (Percy-Smith, 2007). In their 2016 assessment of the UK the UN Committee agreed with the CRAE report that 'children's views are not systematically heard in [UK] policy-making on issues that affect them' and recommended that the UK government:

> establish structures for the active and meaningful participation of children and give due weight to their views in designing laws, policies, programmes and services at the local and national level … Particular attention should be paid to involving younger children and children in vulnerable situations, such as children with disabilities. (UNCRC, 2016, pp 6–7)

Social research and evaluation has an important role to play in enabling children's and young people's views to inform the development of policy, programmes and services. Research and evaluation can provide evidence on what is and is not working, how well it is working, why and for whom. Research and evaluation which actively involves children and young people, if used to inform decision making and policy development, should lead to policies and services that better reflect children's and young people's priorities and concerns. The focus of this book on inclusive approaches will, we hope, ensure that as well as providing robust evidence for policy making and practice, social research and evaluation will reflect the diversity of children and young people and include those who are less frequently heard.

KEY POINTS

- Children's rights are underpinned by the UN Convention on the Rights of the Child (CRC; UN, 1989). The CRC encompasses social, economic, civil and political rights, and asserts children's capacity and right to be involved in decisions which affect them.
- The CRC has informed policy, practice and research agendas which incorporate protection of children and young people and an awareness of their rights to participation in policy, practice and research.
- In traditional research methodologies the perspectives of children and young people were often filtered through the interpretations of adults. However, childhood studies has developed paradigms of children and young people as social actors who can and do have agency and are experts in their own lives.
- Ideas of citizenship position children and young people as members of society with agency, both in their everyday lives and by engaging in collective action towards social change (such as social research and evaluation).
- Although the CRC has not yet been fully incorporated into UK law, the understanding that children and young people should be involved in decisions which affect them has been increasingly reflected in UK legislation and policy.
- There is a need for robust evidence for whether and how these rights are enabled in practice, and whether and when this leads to improved outcomes for children and young people.

• In order to develop policies and services that reflect children's and young people's priorities and concerns, social research and evaluation should seek to actively involve a wide range of children and young people, including those who are less frequently heard.

References

Alderson, P. (2013) *Childhoods Real and Imagined, vol 1: An Introduction to Critical Realism and Childhood Studies.* London: Routledge.

Byrne, B. and Lundy, L. (2015) Reconciling children's policy and children's rights: barriers to effective government delivery. *Children & Society*, 29(4): 266–76.

Children and Families Act 2014 (2014) Available from: www.legislation.gov.uk/ukpga/2014/6/contents/enacted

Christensen, P. and James, A. (eds) (2008) *Research with Children: Perspectives and Practices.* 2nd edn. London: Routledge.

Cockburn, T. (1998) Children and citizenship in Britain: a case for a socially interdependent model of citizenship. *Childhood*, 5: 99–117.

Coyne, I. and Harder, M. (2011) Children's participation in decision-making: balancing protection with shared decision-making using a situational perspective. *Journal of Child Health Care*, 15(4): 312–19.

CRAE (Children's Rights Alliance for England) (2015) *UK Implementation of the UN Convention on the Rights of the Child: Civil Society Alternative Report 2015 to the UN Committee – England.* London: CRAE. Available from: www.crae.org.uk/news/crae-submits-two-child-rights-reports-to-un/

Crowley, A. (2015) Is anyone listening? The impact of children's participation on public policy. *International Journal of Children's Rights*, 23(3): 602–21.

Department of Health (2013) *Chief Medical Officer's Annual Report 2012: Our Children Deserve Better: Prevention Pays.* Available from: www.gov.uk/government/publications/chief-medical-officers-annual-report-2012-our-children-deserve-better-prevention-pays

Devine, D. (2002) Children's citizenship and the structuring of adult–child relations in the primary school. *Childhood*, 9(3): 303–20.

Dockett, S., Einarsdottir, J. and Perry, B. (2011) Balancing methodologies and methods in researching with young children. In Harcourt, D., Perry, B. and Waller, T. (eds) *Researching Young Children's Perspectives: Debating the Ethics and Dilemmas of Educational Research with Children*. Abingdon, Oxon: Routledge, pp 68–81.

Ehrich, J., Pettoello-Mantovani, M., Lenton, S., Damm, L. and Goldhagen, J. (2015) Participation of children and young people in their health care: understanding the potential and limitations. *Journal of Pediatrics*, 167(3): 783–4.

Ferguson, L. (2013) Not merely rights for children but children's rights: the theory gap and the assumption of the importance of children's rights. *International Journal of Children's Rights*, 21: 177–208.

Groundwater-Smith, S., Dockett, S. and Bottrell, D. (2015) *Participatory Research with Children and Young People*. London: Sage.

Hammersley, M. (2015) Research ethics and the concept of children's rights. *Children & Society*, 29(6): 569–82.

Hart, R.A. (2008) Stepping back from 'the ladder of participation': reflections on a model of children's engagement in group activities. In Jensen, B. and Reid, A. (eds) *Progress in Participatory Research with Children and Youth*. Newbury Park, CA: Sage.

Health and Social Care Act 2012 (2012) Available from: www. legislation.gov.uk/ukpga/2012/7/contents/enacted

HM Government (2014) *The Fifth Periodic Report to the UN Committee on the Rights of the Child*. CRC/C/GBR/5 [online]. Available from: http://tbinternet.ohchr.org/_layouts/treatybodyexternal/Download.aspx?symbolno=CRC%2fC%2fGBR%2f5andLang=en

James, A. and Prout, A. (1997) *Constructing and Reconstructing Childhood: Contemporary Issues in the Sociological Study of Childhood*. London: Falmer Press.

Lansdown, G. (2006) International developments in children's participation: lessons and challenges. In Tisdall, K., Davis, J., Hill, M. and Prout. A. (eds) *Children, Young People and Social Inclusion: Participation for What?* Bristol: Policy Press, pp 139–58.

Lansdown, G., Lundy, L. and Goldhagen, J. (2016) The UN Convention on the Rights of the Child: relevance and application to pediatric clinical bioethics. *Perspectives in Biology and Medicine*, 58(3): 252–66.

Lister, R. (2007) Why citizenship: where, when and how children? *Theoretical Inquiries in Law*, 8(2): 693–718.

McNeish, D. (1999) Promoting participation for children and young people: some key questions for health and social welfare organisations. *Journal of Social Work Practice*, 13(2): 191–204.

Mayall, B. (2015) The sociology of childhoood and children's rights. In Vandenhole, W., Desmet, E., Reynaert , D. and Lembrechts, S. (eds) *Routledge International Handbook of Children's Rights Studies*. London: Routledge, pp 77–93.

Moss, P. and Petrie, P. (2002) *From Children's Services to Children's Spaces*. London: Routledge Falmer.

Percy-Smith, B. (2007) 'You think you know? ... You have no idea': youth participation in health policy development. *Health Education Research* 22(6): 879–94.

Percy-Smith, B. (2016) Negotiating active citizenship: young people's participation in everyday spaces. In Kallio, K.P., Mills, S. and Skelton, T. (eds) *Politics, Citizenship and Rights*. Singapore: Springer Singapore, pp 401–22.

Percy-Smith, B. and Thomas, N. (eds) (2010) *A Handbook of Children's Participation: Perspectives from Theory and Practice*. London: Routledge.

Qvortrup, J., Corsaro, W.A. and Honig, M.S. (2009) Why social studies of childhood? An introduction to the handbook. In Qvortrup, J., Corsaro, W.A. and Honig, M.S. (eds) *The Palgrave Handbook of Childhood Studies*. Basingstoke: Palgrave Macmillan

Richards, S., Clark, J. and Boggis, A. (2015) *Ethical Research with Children: Untold Narratives and Taboos*. Basingstoke: Palgrave Macmillan.

Shaw, A., Brady, B., McGrath, B., Brennan, M.A. and Dolan, P. (2014) Understanding youth civic engagement: debates, discourses, and lessons from practice. *Community Development*, 45(4): 300–16.

Smith, C. and Greene, S. (2014) *Key Thinkers in Childhood Studies.* Bristol: Policy Press

Spronk, S. (2014) Realizing children's right to health. *International Journal of Children's Rights*, 22: 189–204.

Tisdall, E.K.M. (2012) The challenge and challenging of childhood studies? Learning from disability studies and research with disabled children. *Children & Society*, 26(3): 181–91.

Tisdall, E.K.M., Hinton, R., Gadda, A.M. and Butler, U.M. (2014). Introduction: children and young people's participation in collective decision-making. In Tisdall, E.K.M., Gadda, A.M. and Butler, U.M. (eds) *Children and Young People's Participation and Its Transformative Potential: Learning from Across Countries*. London: Palgrave Macmillan, pp 1–21.

UN (United Nations) (1989) Convention on the Rights of the Child. Available from: www.ohchr.org/EN/ProfessionalInterest/Pages/CRC.aspx

UNCRC (UN Committee on the Rights of the Child) (2009) General Comment No. 12: The Right of the Child to be Heard. Available from: www2.ohchr.org/english/bodies/crc/docs/AdvanceVersions/CRC-C-GC-12.pdf

UNCRC (2016) Concluding Observations on the Fifth Periodic Report of the United Kingdom of Great Britain and Northern Ireland. Available from: https://tbinternet.ohchr.org/_layouts/treatybodyexternal/Download.aspx?symbolno=CRC/C/GBR/CO/5&Lang=En

Vis, S.A., Strandbu, A., Holtan, A. and Thomas, N. (2011) Participation and health: a research review of child participation in planning and decision-making. *Child and Family Social Work*, 16(3): 325–35.

INVOLVING CHILDREN AND YOUNG PEOPLE IN RESEARCH

Introduction

There are two principal arguments for involving children and young people in research: a rights-based moral argument that it is the 'right' thing to do; and an impact, or evidence-based, argument that involvement has benefits for the children and young people participating, for research and for the services and policies which draw on this research evidence. As discussed in Chapter Two, the United Nations (UN) Convention on the Rights of the Child (UN, 1989) established international recognition that all children have a right to have a say in decisions that affect them. Children's rights and the changing views of the nature of childhood have been reflected, to some extent, in increasing interest in children's and young people's involvement in research (for example, Brady, 2017; Kellet, 2005; Powell and Smith, 2009) both as sources of data and the focus of this chapter, through their active involvement in the research process. In a General Comment on Article 12, children's right to have a say on matters which affect them (see Chapter Two) the UN Committee on the Rights of the Child (UNCRC) outlines how this right should be applied:

A widespread practice has emerged in recent years, which has been broadly conceptualized as 'participation'. This term has evolved and is now widely used to describe ongoing processes, which include information-sharing and dialogue between children and adults based on mutual respect, and *in which children can learn how their views and those of adults are taken into account and shape the outcome of such processes*. (UNCRC, 2009, p 3, emphasis added)

Involving those who are the focus of research has been found to have a positive impact on what is researched, how research is conducted and the impact of research findings on services and in the lives of those involved (Brett et al, 2014; Staley, 2009). Involvement should lead to research, and ultimately services, that better reflect young people's priorities and concerns (Brady et al, 2018b; Fleming and Boeck, 2012). In the past less attention has been paid to the experiences and impact of involving children and young people than to the involvement of adults in research (Bird et al, 2013), and this area is still developing (Parsons et al, 2018).

This chapter covers:

- Why we involve children and young people
- The theory and principles of involvement
- Practical and ethical considerations
- A framework for planning, or reviewing, children's and young people's involvement

Why involve children and young people in social research and evaluation?

Benefits to the research process and validity[1]

Involving children and young people in research can benefit the research by:

[1] Adapted from Shaw et al (2011).

- supporting recruitment of young research participants (and so boosting response rates). For example, involving children and young people can:
  - facilitate access to potential research participants
  - ensure information and recruitment materials are accessible and relevant to their peers
  - enhance the credibility of the study for other children and young people;
- keeping it grounded in the lived experience of children and young people, ensuring that researchers stay mindful of young people's perspectives throughout the process;
- helping to identify appropriate methodologies, or creative and innovative ways of collecting data, that are acceptable to their peers;
- ensuring that research tools are relevant (for example, questionnaires and interview schedules) and issues are approached using language and methods which are accessible and understandable to their peers;
- enhancing the quality and quantity of data gathered – for example, if children and young people are involved in conducting interviews or co-facilitating focus groups, they may put their peers at ease more readily than adult researchers;
- bringing an additional perspective to the interpretation of research findings.

Benefits for the dissemination of research findings include:

- ensuring that the findings are accessible to other children and young people, raising awareness of issues which affect them;
- enabling young people to share their own related experiences, which can have a powerful impact on audiences of all ages.

Benefits for children and young people involved in research

Involving children and young people in research gives them an opportunity to:

- access their right to have a say in decisions that affect their lives, including in research influencing and improving the generation and collation of knowledge on topics of interest to them;
- make an active contribution to their communities and to improve services used by other children and young people;
- develop a variety of transferable skills (for example, in research, presentation, project management, negotiation and decision making);
- extend their social skills and networks, through working with both adults and peers;
- access broader personal development, for example increased confidence, knowledge, self-esteem, and the confirmation that their views matter and can effect change;
- enhance their life and work experience and in turn their CVs;
- gain acknowledgement of their contribution by receiving a payment, reward or other recognition (see 'Key practical considerations' later in this chapter).

Potential wider benefits

- Research involving children and young people, if used to inform decision making or policy formation, is likely to lead to policies and services that better reflect children and young people's priorities and concerns.
- Participative research can offer practitioners new ways of engaging with children and young people.
- It can highlight existing or newly acquired skills and competencies, and lead to greater mutual understanding and respect.
- In organisations where this is not already developed, involving children and young people in research can help to promote a more participative culture.

Theory and principles of involvement

Defining involvement

Before considering how children and young people can be involved in research we need to consider how we define 'involvement'. As the terminology can be contradictory and opaque, with people using different term to refer to the same ideas, or the same terms to refer to different things (Brady, 2017) we start with some key definitions in common use

BOX 3.1: KEY DEFINITIONS

National Institute for Health Research INVOLVE

- **Involvement:** research ... carried out 'with' or 'by' members of the public rather than 'to', 'about' or 'for' them. (INVOLVE, 2018a)
- **Participation**: where people take part in a research study (i.e. participants/ sources of data). (INVOLVE, 2018a)
- **Engagement:** where information and knowledge about research is provided and disseminated (e.g. dissemination, research festivals and open days). (INVOLVE, 2018a)
- **Coproduction**: an approach in which researchers, practitioners and the public work together, sharing power and responsibility from the start to the end of the project, including the generation of knowledge. (INVOLVE, 2018b)

Social Care Institute for Excellence
- **Coproduction** ... involves people who use services being consulted, included and working together with decision-makers from the start to the end of any project that affects them. (SCIE, 2013)

Children's services and child rights
- **Participation:** a process by which children and young people influence decisions which bring about change in themselves, their peers, the services they use and their communities (e.g. Treseder, 1997; Participation Works, 2010).

Wellcome Trust
- **Public engagement:** Helping people access, use, respond to, and create research and innovation. (Wellcome, 2018)

Academic literature
- **Participatory research:** research which engages children and young people as active, informed and informing agents in the research process. (Groundwater-Smith et al, 2015)
- **Participation:** Children and young people taking on higher levels of responsibility than just 'having a say' and 'exercising their agency as active citizens'. (Percy-Smith and Thomas, 2010, p 365)

The definitions in Box 3.1 highlight how different epistemological and methodological traditions can lead to different terminology, and how people can use different terminology to mean the same thing, or indeed the same terminology to mean different things. The key point here is to be aware that when you hear these terms, or others such as 'peer research' or 'co-production', it is a good idea to consider or clarify what is meant, and the values underpinning them.

In this book we mainly use two terms:

- **involvement:** working with children and young people in the design, delivery and dissemination of research (the focus of this chapter), as this is the most commonly used term in a research context.
- **participation:** children and young people as research participants, that is, sources of data (the focus of Chapters Four and Five).

Models of involvement

Now we have defined what we mean by involvement, we go on to consider what this might look like in practice. Although the case for children's and young people's involvement is well established, the forms this should take are sometimes contested, and several typologies have been influential both in promoting children's and young people's involvement and documenting where it is lacking (Tisdall et al, 2014). These typologies have in turn informed a wide range of models, toolkits and 'how to' guides, many of which are referenced in this chapter (or listed in the Bibliography).

Many models of involvement make distinctions according to the degree of power that is shared or transferred. One of the most well-known of these is Arnstein's (1971) ladder of citizen participation (Figure 3.1),[2] which was adapted by Hart (1992) to include children and young people. Hart's (1992) ladder is still central to much discussion about children's and young people's involvement. And the 'degrees of participation' shown in Hart's ladder correspond to definitions of public involvement in health and social care research, which have in the past been defined as a continuum with three points: consultation, collaboration and user-controlled (e.g. Hanley et al, 2004). In this sense:

Figure 3.1: Ladder of participation (adapted from Hart, 1992)

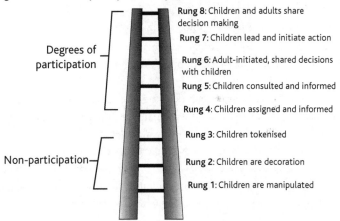

Source: Hart (1992, p 8).

---

[2] Although we have endeavoured to stick to the definitions of 'involvement' and 'participation' defined above, the literature on children's involvement in decision making (not just research) tends to talk about 'participation'. So where we are citing models or quoting directly we sometimes need to use 'participation'.

SOCIAL RESEARCH WITH CHILDREN AND YOUNG PEOPLE

- **consultation** is about asking for children's and young people's views on a particular topic or element of a research project;
- **collaboration** involves a partnership between researchers and children and young people;
- **user-controlled** is when children and young people are fully engaged in and in control of the research (Fleming and Boeck, 2012).

Co-production is also an increasingly popular term in policy making, governance and research (Filipe et al, 2017), as indicated in Box 3.1, and incorporates the definitions of both collaboration and user-controlled research to various extents.

Shier (2001) proposes five levels of involvement in decision making:

1. children are listened to
2. children are supported in giving their views
3. children's views are taken into account
4. children are involved in decision-making processes
5. children share power and responsibility for decision making

Items 1–3 correlate with our definition of 'participation' (being a source of data) and 4–5 with 'involvement': children and young people being directly involved at the point where decisions are made.

The model in Figure 3.2, from National Children's Bureau guidelines, illustrates a clear distinction between research participants (the single circle on the left) and their involvement in the research process (the overlapping circles on the right), which is flexible and can overlap.

> The three interlinked circles illustrate the varying degrees of control that CYP [children and young people] may have in the planning and process of research. The circles are represented as overlapping (and porous), reflecting the fact that – within a single project – the nature of involvement may vary for different children and young people, or at different stages of the research process. (Shaw et al, 2011, p 7)

30

Figure 3.2: Model of children's and young people's (CYP) involvement in research

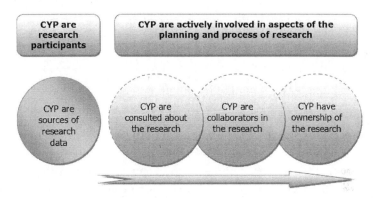

CYP have increasing control of the research process

Source: Shaw et al (2011).

In the models in Figures 3.1. and 3.2, and other models discussed above, consultation is defined as a sub-category of involvement. However, in some models consultation is seen as distinct from active involvement. Hill et al (2004) suggest that consultation is about 'seeking views' and 'being listened to', as opposed to genuinely participatory practice in which children and young people are directly involved in decision making. This chapter focuses mainly on 'collaboration', as defined above, as this is the most common way for children and young people to be involved in social research and evaluation, but we also touch on consultation and young people-led research and provide extensive links to further information in the Bibliography.

Considering inclusion and diversity

As discussed in the introduction to this chapter, we believe that involvement should lead to research, and ultimately services, that better reflect young people's priorities and concerns (Brady et al, 2012; Fleming and Boeck, 2012). But, as discussed in Chapter One, 'children and young people' are far from a homogeneous group; age and other aspects of social background, such as race and ethnicity, disability, social class, family background and use of services all:

> intersect as aspects of who [young people] are, their social position, and what researchers need to consider in designing research approaches appropriate to the young people they wish to involve. (Clavering and McLaughlin, 2010, p 604)

The UN Committee on the Rights of the Child (see Chapter Two) found that 'children's views are not systematically heard in [UK] policy-making on issues that affect them' and recommended that 'particular attention should be paid to involving younger children and children in vulnerable situations, such as children with disabilities' (UNCRC, 2016, pp 6-7). The voices of children and young people who are less frequently heard are often absent from the literature on children's and young people's involvement in research (Richards et al, 2015). For example, users of mental health services (Mawn et al, 2015) and looked after children and young people (Powell and Smith, 2009) are less likely to be involved in research, as are young people with experience of substance misuse services (Brady et al, 2018b).

Involving young people in research: practical and ethical considerations

While many of the considerations and principles for involvement in research are the same for children and young people as they are for adults, particular issues require consideration:

- *How children and young people are involved*: What aspects of research will children and young people be involved in? What level of involvement will they have?
- *What you need to plan for before involving children and young people*: Who to involve? How best to involve them? What are the legal and good practice considerations? How will you evaluate their involvement?

- *Practical considerations*: What resources will you need? How will children's and young people's involvement be rewarded and recognised?

How children and young people are involved

Children and young people can be involved in all stages of the research cycle (see Figure 3.3), from identifying research topics to dissemination of findings. Consider *what stages of your research children and young people could be involved in* as early as possible. It is not always necessary for children and young people to be fully involved in all stages of research, and it can be more appropriate to create 'pockets of participation' (Franks, 2011, p 15), in which the appropriate level of involvement is determined by the circumstances, interests and availability of the young people involved. It may also be that some aspects of the research require particular research skills or experience, or are too challenging or sensitive for children and young people to be involved from an ethical point of view. Involvement does not need to mean everyone doing everything, the important thing is to have the conversations about what children and young people could be involved in, and if there practical or ethical reasons why they cannot be involved in some aspects of research this can be explained to and agreed with the children and young people involved.

As well as considering the stages at which children and young people might be involved you also need to consider *levels of involvement*. As discussed in the previous section ('Theory and principles of involvement'), many models of children's and young people's involvement make distinctions between levels of involvement according to the degree of power that is shared or transferred. Although some of these models imply a hierarchy, Hart argued that the essential elements of the ladder of participation (Figure 3.1) are choice and appropriate levels of support according to children's and young people's developing competence (Hart, 2008). Involvement should be determined by the circumstances of your research project or programme and the children and young people involved (Kirby et al, 2003).

Figure 3.3: The research cycle

Source: Authors.

You should ascertain, and continue to check, the level of involvement desired by individual children and young people rather than assuming any level is level of involvement is inherently 'better' than another (Alderson, 2001). Different forms and levels of involvement may be appropriate in different circumstances and for different children and young people, but in thinking about this it is also important to consider the issues of power and control discussed later in this chapter.

Related to levels of involvement are considerations about *approaches to involvement*. This could include:

- consultation (face to face or online);
- young people's advisory groups (which can be organisation/ project-specific or external, that is, existing young people's research

advisory groups such as those run by GenerationR;[3] see examples later in Box 3.2);
- young advisers (young people who work alongside the researcher team as advisers or co-researchers);
- priority-setting partnerships (see for example the work of the James Lind Alliance);[4]
- co-production (see definitions in Box 3.1);
- peer- or young people-led research (research that is steered and conducted by children and young people with lived experience of the issue being studied);
- user-commissioned research (children and young people are involved in developing a research specification, evaluating submitted proposals and perhaps also advising on and being involved in the research [for example Brady et al, 2011]).

This list is illustrative rather than comprehensive and involvement can include one or more of these elements in different combinations, at different stages of the same research projects. The important point is to consider what would work best for your project and the children and young people you hope to involve.

Table 3.1 illustrates how children and young people (CYP) might be involved in different ways, and at different levels, at each stage of the research process.

BOX 3.2: EXAMPLES OF YOUNG PEOPLE'S INVOLVEMENT

- The GenerationR young people's advisory groups are funded by the National Institute for Health Research and other National Health Service (NHS) organisations and support the involvement of children and young people in the design and delivery of paediatric research in the UK.
- The National Children's Bureau PEAR young people's advisory group worked with the Public Health Research Consortium to advise on and

---

[3] http://generationr.org.uk/
[4] www.jla.nihr.ac.uk/

Table 3.1: Levels and types of involvement

Level of involvement	CYP are research participants	CYP are consulted about the research	CYP collaborate in the research	CYP lead or co-produce the research
Decision making	Researchers in control of all decisions (although individual CYP can decide whether or not to take part)	Researchers take CYP's views into account when making decisions	Decision making shared, or negotiated, between adults and CYP	Researchers provide advice and guidance to CYP and support them to make informed decisions
Developing research idea or proposal, designing and planning research	No involvement (unless participating in pilot study)	CYP may be consulted during development stage	CYP and adults may develop and plan research, or elements of the research, together	CYP initiate research idea and have major influence on design and methodology in some or all of the research
Duration of involvement with the research	At data collection points only	CYP's involvement likely to be sporadic (at key decision-making points)	CYP potentially involved at any or all stages of research	CYP likely to be involved throughout: from conception to dissemination
Research participants, providing data	Yes	Generally not although may have dual role	Generally not although may have dual role	Generally not although may have dual role
Involvement in collection and analysis of data	No	Unlikely, though may be consulted on tools or interpretation of findings	May be actively involved in some aspects (such as designing tools, data gathering, interpretation)	CYP potentially involved in all aspects of the research process
Reporting/dissemination	No involvement. However, findings of research should be fed back to participants if possible	May be asked to comment on draft report or dissemination plans	CYP may have role in report-writing (for CYP audience, for example) and contribute to dissemination activities	CYP may take lead in some reporting and dissemination activities

Source: Adapted from Shaw et al (2011).

- inform research, and developed guidelines for researchers on young people's involvement (PEAR, 2011) and commissioning their own research project (O'Brien and Moules, 2010).
- The McPin Foundation have undertaken a priority-setting partnership with young people to determine priorities for research on child and adolescent mental health.[5]
- Young people were involved in a series of collaborative workshops with adult professionals for an action research project on participation in health care, which resulted in a co-produced participation strategy and a book chapter co-authored with one of the young people involved (Brady et al, 2018a).
- A group of young people with relevant lived experience were involved in a one-off workshop to inform a systematic review on services for people affected by adverse childhood experiences (Lester and Brady, 2018).

A further consideration is *inclusion and diversity*. The dominant structures for children's and young people's involvement in the UK are often groups such as youth councils, forums and advisory groups (Crowley, 2015), and young people's advisory groups can be an effective way to involve children and young people in research. Standing young people's advisory groups, such as GenerationR, as mentioned, offer children and young people a chance to gain skills and experience as well as a chance to contribute to a range of research projects. But they don't work for all children and young people or all research and evaluation projects and can unintentionally marginalise some.

EXAMPLE: INVOLVING LESS FREQUENTLY HEARD YOUNG PEOPLE

The Youth Social Behaviour and Network Therapy (Y-SBNT) study (Watson et al, 2017) was a randomised controlled trial which looked at an intervention currently used in adult alcohol services in the UK to see whether it could be adapted for young people.

The initial plan had been to form an advisory group of young people with lived experience of using substance misuse services, who would travel to regular

---

[5] http://mcpin.org/priorities-for-research-in-children-and-young-peoples-mental-health/

meetings and have ongoing involvement in the study. However, this proved problematic, as many of the young people had complex lives and/or changing circumstances during the course of the study. We found that involvement of 'vulnerable' young people needed to be dynamic and flexible, with sensitivity to their personal experiences and circumstances.

The new approach was a 'hub and spoke' model with a core ongoing group of young advisers, who might change over time, alongside one-to-one and small-group work, and one-off consultations for those young people who were unable to attend group meetings or commit to ongoing involvement (Brady et al, 2018b).

The workshop with young people with lived experience of adverse childhood experiences mentioned in Box 3.2 above is another example of involving less frequently heard young people on a sensitive topic. A blog post on this work gives more information on both the processes and lessons learned (Lester and Brady, 2018).

In seeking to be inclusive, be aware of issues of *power and control*. How and when children and young people are involved is largely determined and controlled by adults (Boyden and Ennew, 1997). It is adult researchers who generally do the asking, the listening and have the power to put into practice (or not) decisions which children and young people are involved in making. The extent to which children's and young people's involvement is active, authentic and ongoing in your research depends both on the approach you choose to take, and whether you are able to create an environment in which children and young people feel comfortable to engage in open and honest dialogue on how they can best be involved. It is important to consider whether children and young people are contributing 'on their own terms and of their own volition ... [rather than being] expected to fit into adult ways of participating' (Cockburn, 2005, p 116).

A further point to note on approaches to involvement is that young people have a right to be involved in matters that affect them, but they also have a right not to be involved (Brady, 2017). Individuals who may be under significant stress might see limited personal benefit to being involved as a research collaborator. It can be particularly difficult to involve children and young people in research on sensitive topics, such as those which are private, stressful or potentially expose stigmatising or incriminating information (Lee, 1993). Inclusive involvement should seek to provide opportunities for any young people who want to be involved to do so in ways that work for them, but also acknowledge that if, when and how they can be involved is ultimately a matter of individual choice.

Planning for involvement

Who to involve and how best to involve them?

As discussed earlier in this chapter and in Chapter Two, consideration is needed on how best to involve a wide range of children and young people in research, including those who are less frequently heard (for example, Brady et al, 2018b). This involves considering:

- *generally*, how to make any involvement as diverse and inclusive as possible within budgetary and other practical considerations;
- whether there are any *specific* considerations in relation to the project or programme in which you want to involve children and young people (for example, do you need to involve children and young people with lived experience of using a particular service, having had a particular health condition and so on), and the children and young people involved.

Once you've decided who you would like to involve you can then think about how best to apply the different levels and approaches discussed earlier in this chapter (in the section 'Theory and principles of involvement') might work best for those children and young people, as well as for your research or evaluation project or programme, as well as identifying the best ways to recruit them. This can be a really useful point to get input from young people with either prior experience of involvement in research, or with particular lived experience (such as Children in Care Councils, young people's groups, disability organisations and so on). Then you can discuss and refine your provisional involvement plans with them.

The role of gatekeepers in involvement

As discussed in Chapter Two (in the section on 'Children's rights'), the involvement of children and young people often includes adults, either parents and carers or professionals, who may as act as 'gatekeepers' and both enable and potentially constrain children's and young people's involvement (Cree et al, 2002). Children and young people can be reliant on significant adults to decide what information they should be given and whether they can be involved (Powell and Smith, 2009). Many children and young people may need adult assistance to enable them to be involved in research (or example, accompanying them to meetings, passing on information and so on). This is more likely if you are seeking to involve children and young people who are less frequently heard, such as younger children and disabled children and young people. Gatekeepers play a significant role in whether and how children's and young people's efforts to be involved are facilitated and supported. They may have reservations or concerns about children's and young people's active involvement in research and 'can also act to exert power over young people to prevent their voices being heard' (Moules, 2005, p 142). So, when planning involvement, it is important to consider how and when you need to engage gatekeepers in order to support the engagement and retention of children and young people.

In thinking about who you want to involve and how, consider:

- whether the research topic or methodology requires specific skills, abilities or lived experience;
- where you might find the children and young people you want to involve (for example, through schools, services, youth organisations, existing children's and young people's groups);
- how to manage the needs, abilities, availability and preferences of the children and young people you want to involve (especially if you will be involving a range of ages and experiences), for example, where and when you will meet them, size of the group, whether involvement will be one-off, ongoing and/or flexible;

- which gatekeepers you will need to engage in order to recruit children and young people and support their ongoing involvement;
- how you will define the young people you wish to involve in project plans and recruitment materials (for example, 'We wish to involve young people aged X to Y with experience of Z');
- how you can be as inclusive as possible in your recruitment (see guidance on accessibility in Chapter Five).

Key practical considerations

Once you have decided who, why and how you need to consider:

- **Resources**: What are the anticipated costs? This might include travel expenses (for children and young people to come to you, parent or carer costs to accompany them or costs for you to go to them); resources including stationery, printing and other materials; room and equipment hire and catering if you are organising meetings; costs of using existing young people's advisory groups (some charge for access); staff time (research and administration); reward and recognition for young people (see later discussion in this chapter).
- **Availability**: Consider the likely availability of the children and young people you want to involve. Ascertain their availability individually once they are involved. Children and young people will generally have school, college and other commitments, so plan involvement around their availability (for example, in evenings, at weekends or in school holidays). Avoid key times of year such as exam periods, if that applies to the age group you are working with, or accept that some young people may have to dip in and out of involvement at busy times (see 'pockets of participation' in the section 'How children and young people are involved' earlier in this chapter).
- **Frequency**: Based on availability and resources as above, as well as the needs of the project, consider how often you will be able to

involve children and young people and how you will keep them engaged in between meetings or other activity.

- **Communication**: Keep in touch with young people in between meetings and other involvement activities, and ask them how they would like to keep in touch. Social media can be helpful (see INVOLVE, 2014) but remember that not all children and young people use email or have regular access to the internet, nor is social media accessible to everyone. For some young people, sending material in the post with SAEs may work best, for others texting or phone calls are preferred. You may also want to produce notes in the form of a newsletter to send young people after meetings and/or with updates on the research project or programme. Ask children and young people what is best for them.

- **Training and support**: Think about the knowledge and skills children and young people will need to adequately prepare them for their role in the project. Allow time for young people to get to know each other if involvement will be through an ongoing group. Keep training accessible, enjoyable and focused on the task in hand. So provide a general introduction to research and/or the project at the start and then provide training as required for different activities. For example, if you're planning to involve children and young people in a literature review do a short session on what a literature review is and then get them to put the learning into practice in the same session. If they're going to be co-facilitating focus groups or interviews do some training on developing topic guides or interview schedules and then get them to role play interviewing each other.

- **Reward and recognition**: Children and young people should be recognised and rewarded for their involvement. There are formal and informal ways to show that young people and children's contributions are valued, including:
  - payment: of money or vouchers;
  - accreditation: for example, through the Award Scheme Development and Accreditation Network (www.asdan.org.uk)

or with the National Open College Network (www.nocn.org. uk);
- certificates: personalised acknowledgement of involvement with details of key activities and achievements;
- references: for college, universities or employers;
- formal acknowledgement: being named on a report or nominated for an award;
- social activities: meals out, outings or group leisure activities. (Adapted from INVOLVE, 2016b)

How you reward children and young people depends on your organisation's policies and processes, available budget and, most importantly, the preferences of the children and young people involved. For further guidance see INVOLVE (2016b).

- **Ending**: Ensure that children and young people involved get copies of key project outputs and updates on what will happen next, as well as a debrief at the end of the project. Plan for the end of the project/children's and young people's involvement. Could you have some kind of celebration (such as an outing) and provide some information on further opportunities?

TOP TIPS: FROM YOUNG PEOPLE

Given that this chapter is about the importance of listening to, and engaging with, children and young people, it is only fitting that we conclude this section with some practical tips, developed by NIHR INVOLVE (INVOLVE, 2016a) in consultation with children and young people involved in research.

1. Don't make assumptions about what we're interested in or what we're capable of – ask us.
2. Our involvement needs to benefit us too – such as by learning new skills, vouchers, payment, activities, meals out, references or having fun.
3. Provide training and support so we can get fully involved – don't just throw us in at the deep end.

4. Give us feedback on what happens after our involvement – show us what difference we're making, so we know our involvement is worthwhile.

5. Use words that we can understand, but without trying to sound young and cool!

6. Involve us in as many parts of the research as possible, from as early as possible and throughout the process.

7. Always provide decent refreshments – not just sandwiches, pizza too!

8. Show respect for our contribution – make us feel included and like an equal part of the team.

9. Find ways to ensure we can all contribute as much as we want to, whatever our age, needs or abilities.

10. We have busy lives and our circumstances, interests and availability might change. Reassure us if we have to miss a session and fill us in afterwards.

11. Organise meetings at times and places that are easy for us to get to and where we feel comfortable.

12. If there is a gap between meetings, keep in touch and give us updates.

13. Communicate with us in different ways such as online, text, social media, phone and post – ask us what we prefer as we don't all use social media or email.

The PEAR (2011) guidelines provide guidance for researchers written by young people.

Legal and ethical considerations

Many of the legal and ethical considerations discussed in Chapter Four also apply to the involvement of children and young people in research, so are not duplicated here. But be aware of:

- **Data protection**: Collect and store information on the children and young people you involve in accordance with the legislation and guidance outlined in Chapter Four.

- **Informed consent**: As with data collection, you need to ensure that you get informed consent from all the children and young people involved in your project, and normally also from a parent or carer if they are under 16 (see Chapter Four). Get rolling consent if children and young people will be involved on an ongoing basis, to avoid having to get consent for every meeting or activity. It is important to stipulate on your consent form that this consent is for the duration of their involvement in the project, and also to regularly review it. Include consent for photos if you think you might want to include these in reports, presentation or future outputs. For informed consent any recruitment materials for involvement should be accessible, clear and interesting. Involving children and young people in developing these materials can be helpful, especially if you have access to young people's advisory groups or other groups of young people with prior experience of research or lived experience of your research topic.

EXAMPLE: CONSENT AND INVOLVING VULNERABLE CHILDREN AND YOUNG PEOPLE

In the Y-SBNT study already mentioned (see Example: Involving less frequently heard young people) signed consent was sought from young people who wished to be involved as young advisers and, in the case of most of the young people under 18, also from their parent or guardian. We were then approached by a project worker from one of the agencies that was helping us to recruit and support young people's involvement, to say that they had a 15-year-old who wanted to be involved in the study, but was estranged from their family and living independently. The young person was keen to take part and requiring parental consent would have prevented them from doing so.

In this instance the issue of consent raised ethical tensions between children's rights to privacy and protection and their right to active involvement. There was a risk, for a young person from a group deemed to be particularly vulnerable, that: 'construct[ing] children and young people's "consent" as somehow lesser than adults is the privileging of particular voices over others' (Richards et al, 2015, p 153).

We followed the National Children's Bureau guidance that consent may be waived 'if seeking parental consent would potentially breach a child's right to confidentiality' (Shaw et al, , 2011, p 27), and also because we did not feel it would be ethical to deny the young person their right to be involved. Involvement was agreed on this basis with a project worker supporting the young person's participation and by the study management group, as well as with the young people involved.

- **Safeguarding**: The involvement lead(s) and anyone else who may be working alone with children and young people involved in the project, group or programme should normally get clearance from the Disclosure and Barring Service (DBS), as well as following safeguarding policies and procedures, see Chapter Four.
- **Confidentiality vs recognition**: There is a balance to be struck between protecting the identities of those involved and crediting them as contributors which needs to be decided on a case-by-case basis in consultation with the children and young people involved. Generally we would advise giving children and young people options around if and how they would like to be credited. But be aware that if you are involving young people in research on sensitive topics and/or because of their lived experience of difficult situations crediting them may leave an online trail which might have future implications they would prefer to avoid.

EXAMPLE: CHOOSING ANONYMITY

In the Y-SBNT study discussed earlier in this chapter, the young advisers chose to remain anonymous:

> 'As much as I would love to put on my CV that I've been involved [in the project] ... people might wonder why I've been an advisor to a drug project ... it just raises a few question marks ... I do always have that worry that they're going to think "Oh she was a druggie" and yes it's the truth but I don't want every employer knowing that stuff.' (Y-SBNT young adviser, quoted in Brady, 2017, p 140)

EXAMPLE: SELECTIVE ANONYMITY

In the project in which young people and health professionals and young people were involved in the co-production of a participation strategy (see Box 3.2, 'Examples of young people's involvement'), the organisation involved wanted to promote the strategy and their involvement in this study. We therefore agreed a further consent process in which people who had ongoing involvement in this study were asked to sign a second consent form (the first was for their involvement in the study) to indicate whether or not they wanted to be credited as a contributor in outputs related to this study. Young people and professionals involved were given the option of being credited by their full name, first name, pseudonym, initials or anonymously as '... and other contributors'.

The resulting acknowledgements included the following:

> The authors of this report would like to acknowledge the [number] staff from [organisation], and the [number] young people who together were involved in the collaborative workshops, meetings and related work during this project. These include but are not limited to: [combination of full and first names of those involved]

- **Reward and recognition**: It is generally considered good practice in public involvement to offer payment (see INVOLVE, 2016b), but be aware of legal restrictions on the times and the amount of hours for which young people aged under 16 can undertake a paid activity. Young people aged 16 and over, and parents and carers, may be in receipt of benefits. Seek guidance on how this might be impacted by a payment for involvement.

Evaluating involvement

There is a need to do more to collate, understand and disseminate robust evidence on the nature and impact of young people's involvement in research and evaluation (Brady and Preston, 2017). Often evidence focuses on the impact on the individuals involved rather than on the impact on the quality and utility of the research itself. When planning your involvement think about how you will evaluate it, document impacts and outcomes and disseminate the learning. This could include:

- Ask children and young people involved to complete evaluation forms and/or evaluation activities, for example activities within meetings or at regular intervals, so that their feedback can inform and improve future involvement. See for example: *Evaluating participation work* (Mainey, 2008).
- If you are running a young people's advisory group or other ongoing involvement, get feedback from researchers who have worked with the group on the impact it had on their work (what did children's and young people's involvement influence or change?).
- Have an end-of-project review including informal critical reflection, or a formal evaluation with focus groups and interviews with children and young people and staff involved.
- Write a journal article or other output on involvement in your project and/or share learning at a conference or other event.
- Involve young people in the evaluation process (for example, helping to define the aims and objectives of the evaluation, developing tools, co-facilitating focus groups, contributing to reports, co-authoring articles and co-presenting at conferences and events).

A framework for involvement

The rights-based framework shown in Figure 3.4 pulls together many of the ideas discussed in this chapter, drawing on our experience of what is needed for children's and young people's involvement to be embedded in research and evaluation in ways that are meaningful, effective and sustainable.

- *Children and young people* are at the centre of the framework because of the centrality of children's rights to this approach, as well as the importance of developing involvement in child and young person-centred ways and in collaboration with children and young people in ways that work for them. So *start with who you want to involve and why*.

- *Scope*: Think about what might enable or limit children's and young people's involvement in your project or programme. *What is the scope for involvement?* What are the policies and processes of the organisation and systems in which involvement will take place? What other factors might enable or limit the forms that involvement can take and who can be involved? For example, the requirements of commissioning and regulatory bodies, gatekeepers including families, carers and support services?

Figure 3.4: A framework for embedding children's and young people's involvement

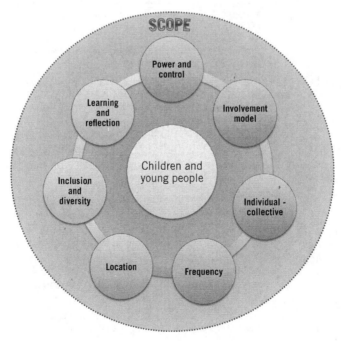

Source: © Brady (2017)

Within 'scope' there is a series of interconnected dimensions (set out in Table 3.2), all of which play a part in determining both what children and young people will be involved in and how they will be involved.

This framework can be used both in planning involvement and in evaluating it. We have used it to work with organisations thinking about how they can best involve children and young people in their work, and for others who want to refine and improve their involvement practice

Table 3.2: Framework dimensions

Dimension	Key questions to consider
Model of involvement	What level and types of involvement are appropriate and possible for the project/programme? At which stages of the research?
Individual– collective	Will children and young people be involved individually, in a group or both?
Frequency	How often does involvement happen? Is it a one-off, does it happen at key points/intermittently or is it ongoing throughout the research process? How will this work best for the project/programme and for children and young people?
Location	Where does involvement take place? In fixed or varied locations, online or in a physical location? Do children and young people come into adult settings or do adults go to young people? Does involvement mean going to pre-existing groups or other forums or establishing new ones, or a combination of both?
Inclusion and diversity	Who needs to be included for the involvement to be meaningful and relevant to the service, organisation or project? Who is and is not currently or potentially included in involvement? What would enable them to be included? What might limit their involvement and can this be addressed?
Power and control	Consider in relation to all of the above: What say do children and young people have in what they are participating in, and how, when and where they participate? (structures and systems) Who decides what is done with the outputs of the involvement? Who evaluates involvement and decides on what the success measures are?
Learning and reflection	How will you evaluate impact and learning from the involvement process

by looking at these dimensions in terms of 'where we are now' and 'where we would like to be'. As discussed, different levels and types of involvement will be appropriate and valid for different children and young people, the nature of the specific research project or programme and the available resources. No level of involvement is 'better' than another, but we hope that this framework and the guidance provided by this chapter will both inspire researchers to involve children and young people in their work, and to do so in ways that are meaningful, effective and inclusive.

KEY POINTS

- **Involvement** means working with children and young people in the design, delivery and dissemination of research, as opposed to **participation**: children and young people as research participants (that is, sources of data).
- Involving children and young people in the research process has benefits for research, the children and young people involved, and is likely to lead to policies and services that better reflect children and young people 's priorities and concerns.
- Children and young people can be involved in all stages of the research process, from identifying research topics to dissemination. Involvement can be at different levels (including consultation, collaboration and co-production) and take different forms. Forms and levels of involvement can vary between and within projects depending on the nature of the research and the interests and availability of the children and young people involved.
- To be inclusive, involvement requires careful consideration, as some approaches may not work for all children and young people and can unintentionally marginalise some.
- The involvement of children and young people often includes adults, typically parents and carers or professionals, who may as act as 'gatekeepers'. They can both enable and potentially constrain children's and young people's involvement.
- When planning involvement consider costs and other resource requirements, children's and young people's availability, how often and where involvement will happen, what training and support will be necessary, reward and recognition, and how you will evaluate involvement.

- Ensure that consent for involvement is ongoing and regularly reviewed. Also check that your consent processes do not unintentionally exclude any children or young people.
- There is a balance to be struck between protecting the identities of those involved and crediting them as contributors, which needs to be decided on a case-by-case basis in consultation with the children and young people involved.
- There is a need to do more to collate, understand and disseminate robust evidence on the nature and impact of young people's involvement in research, on the quality and utility of the research and on the children and young people involved.

References

Alderson, P. (2001) Research by children. *International Journal of Social Research Methodology*, 4(2): 139–53.

Arnstein, S. (1971) A ladder of citizen participation. *Journal of the Royal Planning Institute*, 35(4): 216–24.

Bird, D., Culley, L. and Lakhanpaul, M. (2013) Why collaborate with children in health research? An analysis of the risks and benefits of collaboration with children. *Archives of Disease in Childhood* (Education and Practice edition), 98(2): 42–8.

Boyden, J. and Ennew, J. (1997) *Children in Focus: A Manual for Participatory Research with Children*. Stockholm: Radda Barnen.

Brady, L.M. (2017) *Rhetoric to Reality: An Inquiry into Embedding Young People's Participation in Health Services and Research*. PhD, University of the West of England. Available from: http://eprints.uwe.ac.uk/29885

Brady, L.M. and Preston, J. (2017) *Evaluating the Extent and Impact of Young People's Involvement in National Institute for Health Research (NIHR) Studies: An Assessment of Feasibility*. Report of a project commissioned by the James Lind Initiative. Available from: http://generationr.org.uk/?p=1375

Brady, L.M., Davis, E., Ghosh, A., Surti, B. and Wilson. L. (2011) Involving young people in research: making an impact in public health. In Barnes, M. and Cotterell, P. (eds) *Critical Perspectives on User Involvement.* Bristol: Policy Press, pp 159–68.

Brady, L.M., Davey C., Shaw, C. and Blades, R. (2012) Involving children and young people in research – principles into practice. In Beresford, P. and Carr, S. (eds) *Social Care, Service Users and User Involvement: building on research.* London: Jessica Kingsley, pp 226–42.

Brady, L.M., Hathway, F. and Roberts, R (2018a) A case study of children's participation in health policy and practice. In Beresford, P. and Carr, S. (eds) *Social Policy First Hand.* Bristol: Policy Press.

Brady, L.M., Templeton, L., Toner, P., Watson, J., Evans, D., Percy-Smith, B. et al (2018b) Involving young people in drug and alcohol research. *Drugs and Alcohol Today*, 18(1): 28–38. Available from: https://doi.org/10.1108/DAT-08-2017-0039

Brett, J., Staniszewska, S., Mockford, C., Herron-Marx, S., Hughes, J., Tysall, C. et al (2014) Mapping the impact of patient and public involvement on health and social care research: a systematic review. *Health Expectations*, 17(5): 637–50.

Cockburn, T. (2005) Children's participation in social policy: inclusion, chimera or authenticity? *Social Policy and Society*, 4(2): 109–19.

Cree, V.E., Kay, H. and Tisdall, K. (2002) Research with children: sharing the dilemmas. *Child and Family Social Work*, 7(1): 47–56.

Crowley, A. (2015) Is anyone listening? The impact of children's participation on public policy. *International Journal of Children's Rights*, 23(3): 602–21.

Filipe, A., Renedo, A. and Marston, C. (2017) 'The co-production of what? Knowledge, values, and social relations in health care', *PLOS Biology*, 15(5), p e2001403. Available from: https://doi.org/10.1371/journal.pbio.2001403

Fleming, J. and Boeck, T. (eds) (2012) *Involving Children and Young People in Health and Social Care Research.* London: Routledge.

Franks, M. (2011) Pockets of participation: revisiting child-centred participation research. *Children & Society*, 25(1): 15–25.

Groundwater-Smith, S., Dockett, S. and Bottrell, D (2015) *Participatory Research with Children and Young People*. London: Sage.

Hanley, B., Bradburn, J. and Barnes, M. (2004) *Involving the Public in NHS, Public Health and Social Care Research: Briefing Notes for Researchers*. 2nd edn. Southampton: INVOLVE.

Hart, R. A. (1992) *Children's Participation: From Tokenism to Citizenship*. Innocenti Essays 4. Florence, Italy: UNICEF International Child Development Centre.

Hart, R.A. (2008) Stepping back from 'the ladder of participation': reflections on a model of children's engagement in group activities. In Jensen, B. and Reid, A. (eds) *Progress in Participatory Research with Children and Youth*. Newbury Park, CA: Sage.

Hill, M., Davids, J., Prout, A. and Tisdall, K. (2004) Moving the participation agenda forward. *Children & Society*, 18(2): 77–96.

INVOLVE (2014) *Guidance on the Use of Social Media to Actively Involve People in Research*. Southampton: INVOLVE. Available from www.invo.org.uk/posttypepublication/guidance-on-the-use-of-social-media/

INVOLVE (2016a) *Involving children and young people in research: top tips for researchers*. Southampton: INVOLVE. Available from: www.invo.org.uk/posttypenews/involving-children-and-young-people-in-research-top-tips-and-key-issues/

INVOLVE (2016b) *Reward and recognition for children and young people involved in research: things to consider. Southampton: INVOLVE*. Available from: www.invo.org.uk/wp-content/uploads/2016/05/CYP-reward-and-recognition-Final-April2016.pdf

INVOLVE (2018a) *What is public involvement in research?* Available from: www.invo.org.uk/find-out-more/what-is-public-involvement-in-research-2/

INVOLVE (2018b) *Guidance on Co-producing a Research Project*. Southampton: INVOLVE. Available from: www.invo.org.uk/posttypepublication/guidance-on-co-producing-a-research-project/

Kellet, M. (2005) *How to Develop Children as Researchers: A Step by Step Guide to Teaching the Research Process*. London: Sage.

Kirby, P., Lanyon, C., Cronin, K. and Sinclair, R. (2003) *Building a Culture of Participation: Involving Children and Young People in Policy, Service Planning, Delivery and Evaluation*. London: Department for Education and Science.

Lee, R.M. (1993) *Doing Research on Sensitive Topics*. London: Sage.

Lester, S. and Brady, L.M. (2018) Blog: Involving young people with lived experience of adverse childhood experience (ACEs) in a systematic review. EPPI Centre Blog, UCL. Available from: https://eppi.ioe.ac.uk/cms/Default.aspx?tabid=3681&articleType=Article View&articleId=175

Mainey, A. (2008) *Evaluating Participation Work*. London: Participation Works.

Mawn, L., Welsh, P., Stain, H.J. and Windebank, P. (2015) Youth speak: increasing engagement of young people in mental health research. *Journal of Mental Health*, 24(5): 271–5.

Moules, T. (2005) Research with children who use NHS services: sharing the experience. In Lowes, L. and Hulatt, I. (eds) *Involving Service Users in Health and Social Care Research*. London: Routledge, pp 140–51.

O'Brien, N. and Moules, T. (2010) *The Impact of Cyber-bullying on Young People's Mental Health*. Project report, Anglia Ruskin University, Chelmsford, Essex. Available from: https://arro.anglia.ac.uk/702456/

Parsons, S., Thomson, W., Cresswell, K., Starling, B., McDonagh, J.E. and on behalf of the Barbara Ansell National Network for Adolescent Rheumatology (2018) What do young people with rheumatic disease believe to be important to research about their condition? A UK-wide study. *Pediatric Rheumatology* online journal, 15(53). http://doi.org/10.1186/s12969-017-0181-1

Participation Works (2010) *Listen and Change: A Guide to Children and Young People's Participation Rights*, 2nd edn. London: Participation Works.

PEAR (2011) *Young People in Research: How to Involve Us. Guidance for Researchers from the PEAR Young People's Public Health Group.* Available from: www.ncb.org.uk/resources-publications/resources/young-people-research-guidance-researchers-pear-young-peoples

Percy-Smith, B. and Thomas, N. (eds) (2010) *A Handbook of Children's Participation: Perspectives from Theory and Practice.* London: Routledge.

Powell, M.A. and Smith, A.B. (2009) Children's participation rights in research. *Childhood,* 16: 124–42.

Richards, S., Clark, J. and Boggis, A. (2015) *Ethical Research with Children: Untold Narratives and Taboos.* Basingstoke: Palgrave Macmillan.

SCIE (2013) *Co-production in social care: What it is and how to do it.* Available from: www.scie.org.uk/publications/guides/guide51/what-is-coproduction/defining-coproduction.asp

Shaw, C., Brady, L.M. and Davey, C. (2011) *Guidelines for Research with Children and Young People.* London: National Children's Bureau. Available from: www.ncb.org.uk/resources-publications/resources/guidelines-research-children-and-young-people

Shier, H. (2001) Pathways to Participation: Openings, Opportunities and Obligations. *Children and Society,* 15(2): 107–17.

Staley, K. (2009) *Exploring Impact: Public Involvement in NHS, Public Health and Social Care Research.* Southampton: INVOLVE. Available from: www.invo.org.uk/posttypepublication/exploring-impact-public-involvement-in-nhs-public-health-and-social-care-research/

Tisdall, E.K.M., Hinton, R., Gadda, A.M. and Butler, U.M. (2014) Introduction: children and young people's participation in collective decision-making. In Tisdall, E.K.M., Gadda, A.M. and Butler, U.M. (eds) *Children and Young People's Participation and Its Transformative Potential: Learning from across Countries.* London: Palgrave Macmillan, pp 1–21.

Treseder, P. (1997) *Empowering Children and Young People Training Manual: Promoting Involvement in Decision Making.* London: Save the Children.

UN (United Nations) (1989) *Convention on the Rights of the Child*. Available from: www.ohchr.org/EN/ProfessionalInterest/Pages/CRC.aspx

UNCRC (UN Committee on the Rights of the Child) (2009) *General Comment No. 12: The Right of the Child to be Heard*. Available from: www2.ohchr.org/english/bodies/crc/docs/AdvanceVersions/CRC-C-GC-12.pdf

UNCRC (2016) *Concluding Observations on the Fifth Periodic Report of the United Kingdom of Great Britain and Northern Ireland*. Available from: https://tbinternet.ohchr.org/_layouts/treatybodyexternal/Download.aspx?symbolno=CRC/C/GBR/CO/5&Lang=En

Watson, J., Toner, P., Day, E,. Back, D., Brady, L.M. et al. (2017) Youth social behaviour and network therapy (Y-SBNT): adaptation of a family and social network intervention for young people who misuse alcohol and drugs a randomised controlled feasibility trial. *Health Technology Assessment*, 21(15). Available from: www.journalslibrary.nihr.ac.uk/hta/hta21150/#/abstract

Wellcome (2018) *How we engage the public*. Available from: https://wellcome.ac.uk/what-we-do/our-work/public-engagement

4
ETHICAL CONSIDERATIONS

Introduction

This chapter outlines the key ethical values and principles to consider
when undertaking social research or evaluation with children and
young people and the practical aspects around their application. Rather
than repeating general ethical guidance which applies to all social
research, we focus on the additional issues pertaining to children and
young people, whether this is as research subjects, peer researchers
or co-producers. Ethical considerations are more pronounced when
working with children and young people, partly because of their
relative vulnerability and lack of familiarity with research compared
to adults. However, proportionality is important: the ethical issues
connected to a short survey differ substantially from those involving
in-depth exploration of sensitive data, and not all aspects apply to
every study. Moreover, it is important that ethical considerations are
not used as an excuse to not work with this group. Good planning
and attention to detail are often all that is needed. This chapter covers:

- general ethical foundations and
- additional ethical dimensions and considerations around
  - avoiding harm and providing benefit
  - informed consent

- protecting confidentiality, anonymity and privacy, and
- minimising bias

General ethical foundations

Many excellent references and guidance already exist and most explore the philosophical and pragmatic underpinnings of *good* ethics in social research (see the references section in this chapter and the Bibliography). Applicable to any study with all ages, these tend to agree on a key set of researcher behaviour and characteristics, such as integrity, having the required professional expertise, honesty, openness, reflexivity and treating others fairly; and key principles, including informed consent, preventing harm, creating benefit, using appropriate methods and protecting confidentiality, privacy and anonymity. Examples and summaries of the main points are set out in Box 4.1.

All emphasise that acting 'ethically' involves much more than following a list of do-s and don'ts. In real life research circumstances, ethical principles can sometimes be in tension with each other and it is up to the researcher to balance these conflicts. In other words, guidance alone is never enough and 'cannot replace the need for self-critical, imaginative and responsible ethical reflection about issues which may arise in the course of research, but it can help guide and illustrate how to proceed'.[1]

---

[1] https://esrc.ukri.org/funding/guidance-for-applicants/research-ethics/our-core-principles/

BOX 4.1: EXAMPLES OF KEY ETHICAL FRAMEWORKS FOR SOCIAL RESEARCH IN THE UK

The Academy of Social Science (ACSS)[2]

- Social science is fundamental to a democratic society and should be inclusive of different interests, values, funders, methods and perspectives.
- Social science should respect the privacy, autonomy, diversity, values, and dignity of individuals, groups and communities.
- Social science should be conducted with integrity throughout, employing the most appropriate methods for the research purpose.
- Social scientists should act with regard to their social responsibilities in conducting and disseminating their research.
- Social science should aim to maximise benefit and minimise harm.

The Economic and Social Research Council (ESRC)[3]

- Research should aim to maximise benefit for individuals and society and minimise risk and harm.
- The rights and dignity of individuals and groups should be respected.
- Wherever possible, participation should be voluntary and appropriately informed.
- Research should be conducted with integrity and transparency.
- Lines of responsibility and accountability should be clearly defined.
- Independence of research should be maintained and where conflicts of interest cannot be avoided they should be made explicit.

The Government Social Research Unit (GSRU, 2011):

- sound application and conduct of social research methods and appropriate dissemination and utilisation of the findings;
- participation based on valid informed consent;
- enabling participation;
- avoidance of personal and social harm; and
- and non-disclosure of identity and personal information.

The Social Research Association guidelines include:

---

[2] www.acss.org.uk/developing-generic-ethics-principles-social-science/ academy-adopts-five-ethical-principles-for-social-science-research/
[3] https://esrc.ukri.org/funding/guidance-for-applicants/research-ethics/our-core-principles/

- informed consent
- confidentiality and privacy
- avoiding harm
- research integrity and
- reflexivity

Despite evident overlaps and agreement around core elements, it is also clear from the literature that social research ethical guidelines emerged largely from medical research and are still in development and that there is not one overarching framework covering all professionals conducting social research in the wide range of contexts and settings in which research occurs, including working children and young people (Dingwall et al, 2014).

Research with children and young people can highlight tensions within accepted principles and that historical underpinning. For example, the medical model for informed consent is very helpful, but the social research context is starkly different. It is highly unlikely to involve critical life-or-death decisions, or potentially life-saving treatment, but instead nuanced considerations of 'harm' or what might be in the child's best interests. Weighing up the potential benefits of participation is significantly different in its detail and implications.

Ethical governance and approval

Many agencies have their own internal governance systems to ensure a sound ethical approach in a research project. In addition, some studies require external ethical approval, for example from the relevant local authority, or the Health Research Authority[4] if the research involves NHS patients, staff or premises. Some large UK children's charities offer an ethical overview, guidance and audits, including Barnardo's[5] and the National Society for the Prevention of Cruelty to Children

[4] www.hra.nhs.uk/
[5] www.barnardos.org.uk/what_we_do/policy_research_unit/barnardos_research_ethics_committee.htm

(NSPCC).[6] As well as boosting best practice, getting ethical approval is sometimes a requirement of funders and research bodies also keen to protect the interests of children and young people.

Additional ethical dimensions when doing research with children and young people

Ethical aspects can be more pronounced and awareness more necessary because of power discrepancies, and children's and young people's potential vulnerability, relative limited experience of research and lower awareness of potential risks than adults. As explored in Chapters Two and Three, the power dynamic between the researcher and the researched can be further magnified by differentials of class or education, when covering sensitive topics and when working with vulnerable sub-groups, including children and young people with learning disabilities and those in the care system. The ESRC cautions that these differentials in awareness, experience and power create the potential for exploitation, and discusses the role of gatekeepers in mediating contact and the associated issues this raises around consent.[7]

The main additional dimensions to normal ethical principles are:

- minimising harm and providing benefit;
- ensuring informed consent, autonomy and working with gatekeepers;
- protecting confidentiality, anonymity and privacy; and
- minimising bias.

The following sections cover each of these separately, although in practice they interrelate and overlap. Practical suggestions aim to help you address issues and dilemmas which may arise. That said, it is not feasible to make prescriptions to cover all the potential

[6] www.nspcc.org.uk/services-and-resources/impact-evidence-evaluation-child-protection/conducting-safe-and-ethical-research/

[7] www.ethicsguidebook.ac.uk/Research-with-children-105 (ESRC)

ethical permutations for every research study and the heterogeneity of children and young people. It remains essential for the researcher to be reflexive; ready to adapt key parameters to specific situations and to ability, understanding, background and other variables; and willing to discuss and seek advice around emerging ethical points with colleagues and others.

Not all research studies are the same. The ethics, weighting and emphasis required for a one-off questionnaire to gather feedback on a service used, are very different to those needed for an in-depth study investigating family life or children's health, behaviour, attitudes and development.

Minimising harm and providing benefit

Research with children and young people often requires balancing two core but potentially conflicting principles:

- the opportunity to have their realities and views investigated; and
- avoiding or minimising harm.

Collecting data from adults or other sources may be tempting in terms of more speed, and less cost and hassle. However, if children's and young people's realities, experiences and perceptions are not explored first hand, an important body of evidence remains unknown and they are being denied their right to input into matters which affect them. To enable children and young people scope to exercise their rights, and to generate the best direct data while protecting them from harm, the researcher needs to identify the potential risks involved and develop strategies to address these. On the other hand, beyond minimising harm and in recognition of the altruism involved in participation, the research also needs to provide some benefit for participants.

Potential harm and suggestions on how to minimise

The following are typical 'risks' which can arise. Do not be daunted. The list is not intended to discourage research with children and young people. However, as advised by Alderson and Morrow (2011), assessing potential drawbacks early on helps different parties in assessing if the research is worth doing (including funders) and in planning ways to mitigate any challenges. Not in any order of priority, the most common risks to children and young people are:

- time lost, disruption and impact on opportunities to do other things;
- psychological or emotional distress;
- safeguarding and child protection;
- breach of confidentiality, anonymity or privacy; and
- negative impact from the research or evaluation findings.

Risk: time lost, disruption, opportunities lost to do other things

Research or evaluation involves children and young people giving up time otherwise spent on relaxation, play, study, work or socialising. Participating in research is fundamentally altruistic, as it involves an imposition, regardless of any perceived potential benefits in the eyes of the researcher. Thus it must always be presented as a choice.

Suggestions to minimise this include:
- *respect* children's and young people's time, schedules and commitments;
- *discuss* and negotiate their preferred timings;
- *design* research activities to minimise the time required;
- *acknowledge* and thank them for their time (and pay travel, food and any other out-of- pocket expenses incurred); and
- consider providing some *token of recognition* for the time and effort contributed (discussed under 'benefits' later).

Risk: psychological or emotional distress

Certain topics may be distressing to explore and touch on some issues may be (re-)traumatising for children and young people. To a large extent, this can be anticipated where questions cover issues generally understood to be sensitive, or if the research participants are known to have had difficult life experiences. In addition, distress might seem to arise out of the blue in response to a topic which seemed innocuous. Distress can be difficult or impossible to detect when using certain remote methods, such as self-completion questionnaires.

Distress can emerge in research with people of all ages, but there are additional aspects when working with children and young people. They might not have shared their experience or feelings about it with anyone previously; they may not know that doing so is an option, or who best to talk to, or how to get any support; they may feel upset, but not know precisely what is causing the upset, and be unable to articulate this; they may be less cognisant or confident of their right to remain silent, in other words to not talk about difficult issues during the research; and they may also be less aware of any risks of sharing their memories or emotions with the researcher or within a group. In group settings, the children and young people may be upset by what is raised.

Suggestions to minimise this include:
- Try to *anticipate* topics likely to cause discomfort, using literature and others who know this group or subject.
- Is it *avoidable*? In other words, is it possible to get this data in other ways?
- Anticipate in advance how to deal with distress arising, even if the topics do not indicate that it will.
- *Plan methods* carefully. In general, sensitive topics are best covered using face-to-face methods, to help monitor and respond to any negative impact, but are usually not suited to group discussions. While self-completion questionnaires provide more privacy, the respondent has to deal with any emerging upset alone.

- Use *two facilitators* in focus groups: one can talk to anyone who gets upset individually while the other continues to engage the whole group.
- In group discussions, agree ground rules around respecting others' views and experiences and disclosure.
- *Look out for signs of uneasiness or upset*, even if more difficult to spot in group or remote methods.
- Provide a *'help sheet'* at the end of the session or as part of a questionnaire. This can include details of organisations and other sources of support.
- If using 'remote' tools, such as a self-completion questionnaire, consider seeking feedback on how respondents found completing it.
- If it is essential to cover the stressful topic, or it emerges unexpectedly:
  - be additionally *sensitive* and gentle in questioning;
  - restate *consent* principles, not least that they do not have to talk about this issue if they prefer not to;
  - in a group situation, avoid drawing *attention* to someone's upset, as this might exacerbate the issue and/or generate problems for them later, as well as potentially breach confidentiality;
  - move away from that *topic* for a while and later ask them if they feel able to talk about it again (if it is essential to do so); if not move on;
  - plan extra *time* to go more slowly, allow variations of intensity and more breaks;
  - *breaks* enable you to have a quiet chat to check how they are and ask what they would prefer to do;
  - line up *additional support*, ideally a trusted and suitably qualified person whom they can talk to after the research.

Risk: safeguarding

There are two main and quite different risks here:
- the research or the researcher may pose a risk to the child or young person;

- or the child or young person may raise issues which highlight that they have experienced harm or that they or others are at significant risk of harm.

Broadly speaking, risks usually increase in line with vulnerability, and so are potentially higher for younger children and those with additional needs or living in vulnerable circumstances. Researchers typically work in new contexts and with people they do not already know. Planning and responsiveness are critical.

Suggestions to minimise this:
- Conduct a safeguarding *assessment*, to anticipate risks from others (such as research personnel, other participants and so on) as well as hazards from the research strategy, location and reporting. Then take measures accordingly. For example, fieldwork location and timing can be planned to minimise risks associated with travelling, such as travelling alone at night-time.
- Use or adapt your own *child protection policy* to cover this piece of research, or create a policy. Liaise with agencies where you will conduct the research (such as schools, children's homes and so on) and agree to work within their policies. Such policies cover what to do if someone makes a disclosure, or if concerns emerge about their own or someone else's safety. If your organisation does not have one, the NSPCC provides excellent guidance on developing and writing a child protection policy.[8]
- Provide *training* around safeguarding and child protection to all fieldworkers. The NSPCC provides online training[9] and local Safeguarding Children's Boards and other local agencies can advise on training available locally.

[8] www.nspcc.org.uk/preventing-abuse/safeguarding/writing-a-safeguarding-policy/
[9] www.nspcc.org.uk/what-you-can-do/get-expert-training/child-protection-introduction/

- Ensure researchers who will have direct contact with children and young people have an up-to-date enhanced criminal record check completed by the *Disclosure and Barring Service*.[10] Note these checks are retrospective, only report on records held by the UK police and are not unassailable.
- Minimise the *time* researchers spend alone with a child, for instance in an interview.
- Explore working in *pairs* of researchers (unless it would be too intimidating for a child); and/or with friendship pairs of children or young people (while balancing this with confidentiality).
- When working with very young or disabled children it may be necessary for the *parent or carer* to help or be close by to oversee their safety. One option is to use a room with a window, or sit at either end of a largish room, so that the parent or carer can keep an eye on things, but not talk for the child.
- If adults have to be very closely involved, for example to interpret or provide other assistance, questions may need to be adjusted, to help protect the child's or young person's confidentiality, as there may be matters which they prefer not to discuss so openly.

Risk: breach of confidentiality privacy or anonymity

Children, young people and others may not always appreciate the risks to their confidentiality, privacy or anonymity. The section 'Protecting children's and young people's confidentiality, privacy and anonymity' in this chapter covers these matters in detail, along with the interface with safeguarding.

Risk: impact and scope of findings

'Negative' findings may rebound on research participants, and could exacerbate an existing *demonology* around their age-group. It is not unusual for research data to be misreported in the media and for

[10] www.gov.uk/government/organisations/disclosure-and-barring-service

nuances to be overlooked in a snappy title. Moreover, this vulnerable group has little public voice or right to reply.

Suggestions to minimise this:
- There is arguably an extra obligation on researchers to *anticipate* how reports could be misconstrued and to write accordingly.
- *Involving* children and young people for example as research advisers, might improve the presentation of findings.

There is also a risk of excessive expectations of the research, and disappointment that it does not achieve more. Most children and young people have little experience of research and so might accept claims made, especially to boost recruitment.

Suggestions to minimise this:
- be honest
- clarify whenever possible what can and cannot be reasonably expected from this research.

Providing benefit

Minimising harm is only one side of the coin. A major ethical underpinning of any social research study is to provide benefit. As well as benefitting society as a whole, for example by increasing knowledge or improving policy, it is worth exploring what participants get in return for giving their time and data to a research.

Suggestions on some benefits to integrate include:
- Plan the research activities to be as *enjoyable and fun* as possible.
- Provide *learning opportunities*. This can range from training in research activities, or skills such as photography, or public speaking, or something complete tangential, such as football skills.
- If working through or with existing institutions, consider proportionate benefits to provide the *whole group*. This could include

funding a new service, play staff, a trip out, or a new activity or resource.

• Consider the scope to provide a *thank you at the end of fieldwork*, and any ethical factors around same. On the one hand this can serve as recompense for the disruption involved, but can carry risks too. For example, it could bias the sample of those willing to participate, or responses: as participants may feel more compelled to provide positive answers. Morrow (2009) advises clarifying the criteria and justifications for any rewards or payment to be made. If financial rewards are considered ethical and appropriate, they can be per individual, or given to the whole group. High street shopping vouchers are common. However, sometimes a cash payment might be more ethical, for example to enable people on low incomes to choose where to shop. For young children any monetary reward is usually given to parents/ carers. INVOLVE (2018) provides some ideas on suitable rewards for involvement.

TOP TIPS: MINIMISING HARM AND PROVIDING BENEFIT

• Conduct a simple but comprehensive risk assessment during research planning.
• Discuss plans with others more experienced in working with younger age-groups.
• Recognise the diversity within the group.
• Agree a safeguarding policy and process with partner agencies and all fieldworkers.
• Consider what benefits participants could get from the research without creating or aggravating bias.

Informed consent

This fundamental principle deserves additional consideration when the research or evaluation includes children and young people, partly because of potential questions around their capacity to appreciate potential consequences and thus their ability to give valid consent, as well as the common need to work with gatekeepers. Different methodologies generate distinct dilemmas and implications for the consent process. Here the main parameters around valid consent when working with children and young people are set out separately, although in real life they are interconnected.

This section covers:
- autonomy
- capacity, age, cognitive ability and competence to consent
- working with gatekeepers
- opting in and opting out
- information requirements
- recording consent
- timing of seeking consent
- specific consent considerations when using different research methods

Autonomy

Autonomy is the bedrock underpinning the principle of voluntary consent in research. Autonomy refers to a person's right to make their own decisions, without being coerced. It is closely intertwined with dignity, which can be defined as someone's sense of self-respect and self-worth. Violations of autonomy include objectification, deception, or treating someone mainly as a source of data.

Autonomy is closely entwined with *gatekeeping*: even if gatekeepers give permission, the child or young person *retains their autonomous right* to consent or not for themselves. To put this another way, involving gatekeepers does not reduce the obligation to seek consent directly from the child (and respect that decision).

Although all social research guidance holds that children are autonomous and that their autonomy to give or withhold consent to research should be respected, ensuring this in practice may require a bit more thinking and effort. For a start, most children and young people have little experience of research; and are generally accustomed to doing what they are told by adults. During research, adults (parents, teachers and other professionals) also act as gatekeepers. It can be additionally difficult for a child or young person to assert their autonomy and refuse consent, more-so when others (gatekeepers) have already given the go-ahead. For a child, refusing consent may take many forms and may not be a simple '*no thank you*'. It is as likely to be expressed indirectly and/or physically.

Judging when a young child is acting autonomously can be difficult. For example, they may be used to being compliant and/or may want to say 'yes' because their friends did. Much depends on how the research is explained. Repeatedly emphasising that participation is voluntary, reaffirming their autonomous rights and showing respect for whatever decision they make, will help. Starting the research session with a short warm-up activity can be used to demonstrate your respect for their decisions.

Capacity, age, cognitive ability and competence to consent

A child's cognitive ability to comprehend what is being asked and what participating in research might entail for them is critical to valid consent. Although the contexts are quite different, the principles are borrowed from medical case law (General Medical Council, 2018).[11] In contrast to a medical intervention, such as surgery, asking a child to give their opinions in say a questionnaire usually carries less potential harm, but equally brings fewer, if any, benefits. In practice, competence to consent is closely linked to age, the complexity and importance of the decision to be made, any associated risks, and the accessibility of the information provided.

In terms of *age* alone:
- Once a young person turns 16 they are presumed to have full capacity to consent in their own right and count as 'adults' for

---

[11] Mainly called 'Gillick competence', from the case *Mental Capacity Act 2005; Gillick v West Norfolk and Wisbech AHA* [1986] AC 112.

research purposes, unless they come under mental capacity legislation, which is covered later.

- For those under 16, there is no absolute age at which a child becomes 'competent'. This varies. What matters is the individual's maturity and ability to understand what is being asked of them and to weigh up the likely benefits, risks, disadvantages and other consequences.
- For internet-related research, such as the processing of personal online data from a website, the Data Protection Act 2018[12] stipulates that a child must be 13 or over to be counted as competent to give consent, and that in most cases for children under 13, consent must be sought from whoever holds parental responsibility for them while also stipulating some exceptions, including emotional counselling. Social research practice uses the age of 16 as the threshold for seeking parental permission first in most cases.

Cognitive ability to appreciate complexity, consequences and abstractions generally increases with age. Physical age is only one yardstick. Children develop at variable rates and have different life experiences, educational and other inputs. While there is no absolute age at which a child becomes capable, for practical purposes most children and young people can be expected to handle more complicated concepts and details and remember more as they get older. In other words, what children aged 5, 8, 10 or 14 can be expected to comprehend will differ, as will the methodological expectations on them and the reliance on gatekeepers.

Most of the rest of this section covers children under 16, but some of the considerations may sometimes be worth applying to older young people, if there are any concerns about their capacity to understand what the research might involve.

---

[12] Article 8 of the GDPR (General Data Protection Regulation)and Data Protection Act 2018: https://ico.org.uk/for-organisations/guide-to-the-general-data-protection-regulation-gdpr/children-and-the-gdpr/what-are-the-rules-about-an-iss-and-consent/

Creating accessible information for consent purposes

Capacity and accessibility are closely intertwined. Reams of detail and technical jargon obscures meaning. Information and consent processes need to be made accessible and match an individual's level of comprehension and any additional needs. In practice, the researcher needs to ascertain each individual's capacity to weigh up the information about the research and any potential benefits and risks it may hold for them in order to give or withhold valid consent. Designing information that is accessible and inclusive requires additional attention when working with:

- very young children (babies to age 6 or 7);
- disabled children and young people; and
- children, young people and gatekeepers who do not speak English as a first language.

Working with gatekeepers

It is normal to work with gatekeepers when conducting research or evaluations with children and young people. Gatekeepers fall into the following broad groups and roles:

- those who have '*parental responsibility*' and whose role and duty is to safeguard and protect the best interests of the children and young people *under 16* in their care (including parents, guardians, the local authority/social worker and possibly foster carers);
- those who *work with children or young people* and can help researchers make contact with them (this overlaps with, but is wider than, above and includes teachers, youth and other service providers); and
- parents, carers and professionals who work with children and young people who have additional needs and can help you understand those needs and how to adapt the research and information materials and processes to make these *accessible*.

As discussed in Chapter Two, a priority for parents and other gatekeepers is protecting the child or young person. As part of this, they need to *weigh the benefits and risks* of any research with the child's or young person's best interests. Gatekeepers may have a better grasp than the child of the hassle or commitments that the research would entail; potential risks to confidentiality or anonymity; possible long-term impact; as well as the appropriateness of the methodology. Working with gatekeepers involves a delicate balance between respecting the child's or young person's autonomy as well as the responsible adult's role to protect their well-being. Nonetheless, the child's autonomy remains intact. Gatekeepers help to inform the child or young person and effectively grant the researcher permission to approach the child, provide information and seek consent directly from them. The child retains the ultimate right to grant or withhold consent, and to change their mind at any time.

As a rule of thumb, the role of gatekeepers *increases with both the degree of intrusion, risk* and *potential harm* related to the research in question, and with the *vulnerability* of the child or young person. It decreases as the child's or young person's comprehension, abilities and competence to determine what is in their best interests increase, and when the risk of harm is minimal. The parents of children and young people with some learning disabilities may have to act as gatekeepers in more instances and for longer than other parents.

When doing research with children and young people who need additional support to give informed consent, it is best practice to work *closely with them and their gatekeepers* to get a better understanding of abilities and needs and how best to make information pertinent and accessible, as well as any overall research methodology.

Some people have *layers* of gatekeepers (see Figure 4.1). For example, in a school setting, the head teacher, parents and maybe also the local authority must grant permission to carry out the research within the school and collect data from pupils. For children in the care system, parental responsibility usually lies with either the local authority or the birth parents, but sometimes with foster carers.

Figure 4.1: Example of layers of gatekeepers

Making contact with an 11 year old in a youth group

Child lives with birth parents   **Looked after child in foster care**

Note: PR – parental responsibility
Source: Authors

Each gatekeeper needs similar details about the research, as well as any implications. This generally includes the research aims, purpose and any value; practical details on how it will be conducted safely and ethically and not create a disproportionate imposition on participants; proof of Disclosure and Barring Service (DBS) clearance; and possibly approval from a higher body, such as a local authority, and/or ethical approval.

Each gatekeeper helps *explain and broker* the research to the next, and eventually to the research participant. Each is critical in ensuring the research is explained correctly. In practice, some bits of information and the principles of voluntarism and autonomy can easily get lost along the way and need re-emphasising to each party.

EXAMPLE: NUMEROUS GATEKEEPERS

A research study about experiences of the care system included focus groups with looked after children and young people. The gatekeepers whose permission was sought included five local authorities, social workers, foster carers, a local charity that provided after-school services for looked after children (and which hosted the focus groups) and in some cases the children's birth parents.

When it may be more ethical to not seek parental permission

Exceptionally, the research subject may make it more ethical to not contact those with parental responsibility in relation to a child under 16, in the interests of minimising harm. For example, a child or young person may attend a service which provides emotional counselling, or supports children who are experiencing domestic violence, or who want to discuss their sexual identity. If their parents are unaware they use this service, alerting them to that fact may create a problem, or danger, for the child or young person, and would override their autonomy to disclose this matter when they want to.

Some young people, under 16, live independently and may be estranged from those with parental responsibility. Contacting a parent in such a situation may create a risk or simply be unfeasible. As well as assessing the child or young person's competence to understand the implications, weigh up the risks and benefits and consent for themselves, it is advisable to discuss a dilemma like this with others. Check if there are any adults, such as professionals, who know the child well, conduct extra risk assessments and seek ethical guidance.

Figure 4.2: Age, gatekeeping and mental capacity

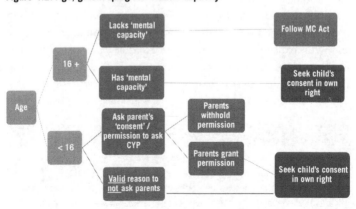

Source: Authors

EXAMPLE: NOT SEEKING PARENTAL PERMISSION

A young person aged 15 lived independently as they were estranged from their family. While a support worker acted as a gatekeeper, it was not feasible or safe to contact anyone who had legal parental responsibility. As the young person wanted to take part in the research, and was judged by the support worker and research team as competent to understand the issues involved and to give informed consent, it was considered more ethical to include them than to deny their right to participate.

Young people over 16

For social research, 16 is generally taken as the age of maturity. Therefore, once a young person turns 16 a gatekeeper's permission is no longer necessary, as long as they are not 'mentally incapable'.

However, in practice you may still need others' help to contact and recruit young people aged 16 and older, advice on making information and tools accessible, and help with research venues. And in some complex research projects it might also be best practice to involve practitioners, parents or carers to independently advise the young person on long-term considerations.

Young people aged 16 and over who are '*severely mentally impaired*' and deemed to lack '*mental capacity*' are covered by the Mental Capacity Act 2005 and associated official guidance.[13] One of the criteria required for their inclusion is to show that research of comparable effectiveness could not be carried out if the sample was confined to those who have capacity. If a person is deemed to lack the capacity to consent, but their participation is considered essential, the researcher must apply for formal ethics approval and seek advice about their participation from their carers. Official guidance also sets out other detailed steps to ensure their protection.

---

[13] Mental Capacity Act England 2005; Adults and Incapacity (Scotland) Act 2000; NHS guidance: Mental Capacity Act: www.nhs.uk/Conditions/social-care-and-support-guide/Pages/mental-capacity.aspx) and www.shef.ac.uk/polopoly_fs/1.165638!/file/SREGP-Adults-LCC.pdf.

Opt-in consent processes versus opt-out

This has additional considerations when working with younger groups.

- **Opting in** is where potential participants are invited to volunteer to be in the sample for a specific study. For example, an invite is pinned on a public notice board (physically or online). An opt-in becomes more expected as the potential levels and impact of involvement, or risks of harm, increase, such as research covering sensitive topics or involving intrusive methods. However, response rates among children can be low and can be influenced by many factors, some unintentional. For example, opting in relies on literacy and language skills and many children and young people might not see the notices for different reasons. Last but not least, children and young people less familiar with research are less likely to volunteer, which would bias a sample.
- **Opting out** is where people are initially included in the first sample or long-list, but are then given the opportunity to *not* to take part in the research. In surveys, the decision to complete a questionnaire or not also provides another opportunity to opt-out. An opt-out is more useful to researchers trying to target a specific population or sub-group, which may be less likely to respond to an opt-in.

In real life, these distinctions are blurred and intertwined with children's and young people's levels of understanding, autonomy and potential vulnerability as well as the researcher's scope to contact them. Whatever approach is used, researchers need to bear in mind the potential confidence issues involved and the greater vulnerability of younger participants and actions needed to exercise real choice. Saying 'no' to a professional, such as a researcher (as in opting out) takes a lot of self-assurance and may also risk attracting undesirable attention. A child might not feel confident enough to opt in or out if their friends are doing the opposite. If parents take an initial decision, does a child feel they have a chance to either opt in or out?

In practice both options are commonly combined, with initial opt-out stages, followed by a discrete opt-in process. Each stage enables more detail to be explained.

Information necessary to underpin consent

When seeking consent, the person being asked needs to be able to easily understand what the study is for, who is doing it, what participation might entail and any potential risks. In practice, the researcher is looking for agreement to each aspect, including: the methods, topics, timing, location, recording, data processing and reporting. Unless the information is clear and accessible, consent cannot be valid.

The challenge is in finding a balance between conveying enough detail to enable a child or young person to make a meaningful decision and give valid consent if they want to, while ensuring the information is accessible, comprehensible and not overwhelming. Children and young people will vary in their capacity to consent to each of the detailed aspects. For example, while most will understand what it means to give their view on a topic, the nuances of data protection may be unintelligible and long-term matters immaterial. The consent process and information need to take account of children's competence to comprehend relevant risks and determine how much to rely on gatekeepers.

Information methods

Even if written information is provided, the research always needs to be explained verbally too, at least at every encounter, to each gatekeeper and to each young participant. This helps check consistency of understanding and address queries.

Written information is only suitable for children who are reasonably literate. This does not correlate with a precise age. But, in general, written materials would not be suitable for most children under 8 and older again for children who have additional needs around literacy.

If literacy is in question, relying on written information would make consent invalid.

Written information needs to:
- suit a range of abilities – one version is ideal, usually the one that requires least literacy;
- be brief, straightforward, accessible and proportionate, but not patronising;
- use direct language and avoid technical terms or research jargon;
- use common short words and brief sentences;
- avoid research terms, slang and resist temptations to sound on trend;
- be legible use at least 12 or 14 point fonts;
- use a high contrast, such as black or dark blue on a light background. However, like other aspects, this will vary and some people will find other colour combinations easier to read;
- use graphics and other visuals sparingly.

Sometimes a short video or smartphone application, explaining the research, is a useful option, if budgets allow. This may be more accessible than written information and the child or young person can revisit the film as often as necessary to remind themselves about the research and consent.

Layering the information so that more details are provided in successive stages improves accessibility. It may help to use certain *formats* for information and consent materials, for example using Easy Read,[14] large type or braille. The Department of Health (2010) and many UK disability organisations, such as Mencap,[15] the National Autistic Society, Royal National Institute of Blind People (RNIB) and the National Deaf Children's Society,[16] are examples of useful agencies

---

[14] www.bild.org.uk/resources/easy-read-information/
[15] www.mencap.org.uk/advice-and-support/health/accessible-information-standard
[16] National Deaf Children's Society (NDCS) (nd) *How to Make Your Resources Accessible to Deaf Children and Young People.* London: NDCS. Available from: www.ndcs.org.uk/document.rm?id=9325

which can provide helpful advice and resources. Working closely with gatekeepers, such as parents or carers, helps understand an individual's or group's accessibility needs. Get others to test any information and consent forms produced, ideally children and young people of the target age and abilities. Better still, ask a group of representative children or young people to help design suitable information tools with you.

If you need to get information materials translated in to other languages, use a good translation service and test the results on someone else. DIY and online translation can result in some dreadful errors!

Layering information

Delivering information in stages and 'layers', in other words providing additional details over time, helps avoid overburdening and confusing potential participants with a daunting wodge of detail, especially if the topic or the consent process is complicated. Layering assists accessibility and can help in recruiting those unfamiliar with research. Initial information can provide a summary and what would be expected of participants (such as a half-hour discussion about travel, to be held at their school). Later, more details can be provided about the processes, methods, topics and data protection. Voluntarism and the right to change their mind without giving a reason needs to be included at each stage.

EXAMPLE: LAYERING OF INFORMATION AND GATEKEEPING

The researcher needed to recruit primary and secondary school pupils to take part in focus group discussions about local school transport options, attitudes and behaviour. An opt-out approach was used for schools. In other words, specific schools were invited because they met certain criteria.

In the schools which agreed to take part, a letter was written to parents, to seek their agreement to approach their children. This was sent to parents by the school administrator. Therefore, the researcher had no need to be given any personal data.

Given the perceived low risk attached to this study, not least the low likelihood of sensitive topics being discussed, this letter was an opt-out: parents were asked to state if they did not want their child to take part.

The discussion groups were planned to take place within class groups. Teachers were given information to read out and to give out to pupils, along with some frequently asked questions and answers. This included more information about the research purpose and methods, and examples of the questions.

When the researcher first met the teachers and pupils, they explained the study and emphasised individuals' right either to not be involved at all or to not answer specific questions. Pupils were also able to choose to do another activity while the research was going on if they chose not to participate. This had been previously arranged with the head teacher and teachers.

Checking and recording consent

The Data Protection Act 2018 requires the consent process to be recorded, including what information and details were provided to whom, the date and time, and the researcher's name. As many children and young people have gatekeepers, it might be good practice to record this and any variation in the information given to them.

Whether or not it is best to ask someone to sign a consent form has to be balanced with several factors, such as the sensitivity of the topic; methods; the number of agencies and fieldworkers; and whether ethical approval is needed. In addition to providing information in writing and verbally, having a standard information sheet with some boxes which a person individually ticks as they read it can double as a checklist to ensure that fieldworkers relay information consistently. However, a tick-box form is insufficient on its own[17] It is essential also to check verbally (if feasible) how well the information has been understood and explain more as needed.

Moreover, there is a risk that signing a consent form is perceived as a binding contract, making people feel more obliged to stay in the

---

[17] ICO (Information Commissioners Office) guidance on the Data Protection Act 2018, https://ico.org.uk/for-organisations/guide-to-the-general-data-protection-regulation-gdpr/consent/how-should-we-obtain-record-and-manage-consent/

study, which undermines the principle of voluntary consent (Graham et al 2007).

When to seek consent

Timing is another major consideration in research with children and young people. If consent is sought too far in advance, they may have forgotten what they consented to by the time the research happens. Be prepared to repeat information and check that they are still happy to proceed, regardless of any consent given previously.

Treating consent *as a live and ongoing dynamic* is critical. Even if a child or young person gave consent initially, their continued consent needs to be checked throughout the research activity, not least because of the power dynamics, combined with lack of confidence, the possibly that they did not really understand what was being asked of them or what it would entail to begin with, and a tendency to be polite and to follow what their peers are doing.

At the start of any data collection process, remind them that participation is totally voluntary, that they do not have to answer any question if they do not want to, and that there will be no detrimental consequences if they need a break, or want to stop altogether.

Regardless of earlier consent, the researcher needs to be alert to *physical or other clues* that the person wishes to stop, in other words wants to vary or withdraw their consent. It is important to *actively look for any indirect signs of discomfort* or unease. These include becoming more active, or distracted, fidgeting, asking for breaks, not answering questions, being monosyllabic, or giving lots of '*I don't knows*' as answers. Being observant, flexible and responsive are crucial, as is working closely with carers. Be prepared to stop, offer a short a break, vary the activity, or change the types of questions, ask if they are happy to proceed, and so on.

EXAMPLE: ENSURING ONGOING CONSENT

In a focus group with a small group of looked after children, all seemed happy chatting (and drawing) until the subject of foster carers getting ill arose out of the blue. The atmosphere changed immediately and the children became restless and less talkative. The researchers asked if they would like a break and some snacks, to which the children readily agreed. During the break the conversation was deliberately kept to innocuous topics. After a while the children were asked if they wanted to resume and if so if they would prefer to talk about something else. They all agreed on that basis.

After the group the carers and social workers were told about what had happened, in terms of the topic which sparked distress and the children's reaction, so that the carers could look out for any longer term impact.

Specific consent considerations when using different research methods

Because of potential vulnerability and lower levels of confidence and awareness of consequences, it helps to bear the following in mind.

- *Online, paper and other self-completion questionnaires* usually include information about consent. But literacy is a challenge and researchers should avoid giving overwhelming details. If a survey is administered by third parties, or completed alone, it is impossible to ascertain how well the information relating to consent has been understood, or to clarify any aspects.
- *Individual face-to-face interviews* provide lots of scope to explain the study in as much detail as needed, to match the child's or young person's abilities and comprehension, answer questions and clarify that participation is voluntary. It also enables ongoing observations to look for non-verbal cues. However, the personal interface with the researcher contains a power dynamic, which may make a child more hesitant to ask to stop. Agreeing a non-verbal method in advance can help, such as holding up their hand or a card.

- *Focus groups* also enable ongoing observation. Nonetheless, exerting individual autonomy involves standing out from the crowd and can be challenging and embarrassing. Viable and safe ways to withdraw consent need to be anticipated, practicable and safe, such as agreeing certain signals and providing an alternative activity.
- *Observations*: As well as the risk of creating bias, whether covert or overt, there is a risk of including other children and young people who have not given consent.
- *Using social media and the internet*: At the time of writing, internet-based surveys are quite common. However, the use, benefits and parameters of social media, such as online surveys or fora (Facebook and Twitter being current examples), for social research purposes are still being explored and ethical guidelines being developed. For example, Young Digital[18] and the British Psychological Society (2017, p 9) refer to additional difficulties in ensuring valid informed consent: that children and young people appreciate what information is held in public or private arenas; and that additional consent and confidentiality issues may emerge in relation to using commercial online tools, or if data is processed by third parties.

The Government Social Research Unit's guidelines (GSRU Social Media Group, 2016) provide some outline ethical principles around online research methods. This points to the need to have a clear research case to collect this type of data; the challenges in getting explicit consent; and potential compromises around confidentiality, privacy and anonymity.

The Data Protection Act 2018 emphasises that explicit consent must be sought from whoever holds parental responsibility for a child under 13 before they can consent to use online services, as much as this is practicably possible in an online situation. Some exceptions are allowed, for example if using an online emotional counselling service. This includes using an online platform such a Facebook as a medium

[18] www.youngdigital.net/

for conducting a survey.[19] As social researchers normally seek initial parental permission for those under 16, the 13-year-old provision may only be an issue in only a small number of cases. The parameters of the new rules in relation to research alone will become clearer over time. Seeking ethical guidance and clearance around this is advisable.

The Market Research Society (MRS), in its 2012 guidance, cautions against using only email as a means of seeking consent from a child or young person, especially as email is not secure. They recommend using a paper letter and/or phone call. If a researcher participates in an online forum the MRS recommends that they:

> declare their presence, their role as a researcher, the identity of the organization they work for, what information they intend to collect, what it will be used for and who will have access to it. It is not acceptable for a researcher to ... to passively collect data without prior consent. (Market Research Society, 2012)

The British Psychological Society (2017, p 9) recommends spreading the information about the purpose of the study, throughout an online tool, and using check boxes to help ensure respondents have read the information.

---

[19] https://ico.org.uk/for-organisations/guide-to-the-general-data-protection-regulation-gdpr/

TOP TIPS: INFORMED CONSENT

- Demonstrate respect for autonomy. Prove you mean what you say.
- Explore the precise capacity of your target group(s) to understand the information and consent in their own right.
- Identify what support they need to do so.
- Adapt information materials and language to cognitive skills and literacy levels. Work with children, young people and gatekeepers to ensure materials are accessible.
- Approach consent as an ongoing and continuous process.
- Provide information in staged layers if possible and be prepared to repeat.
- Observations can be better than relying on words in gauging if a child is happy to proceed.
- Work closely with gatekeepers.
- Remind all gatekeepers (politely) that their approval does not obviate the need to seek consent directly from young participants.
- Different methods allow for different consent processes. Each carries discrete challenges.
- When using online methods, consider proportionate ways to ensure valid consent.

Protecting children's and young people's confidentiality, privacy and anonymity

Respecting and protecting children's and young peoples' confidentiality, privacy and anonymity are essential to protecting their rights and welfare. The research may also impact on the confidentiality of others, such as peers, parents, family and friends. There is also a balance to be struck between confidentiality and child protection: if concerns emerge it can be ethically appropriate to breach confidentiality. Researchers need to anticipate and explore the potential confidentiality issues in the planning stages and design ways to address them.

EXAMPLE: DEFINITIONS

Protecting **confidentiality** means handling and processing all personal data in a confidential way and ensuring that these details remain protected throughout all stages of the research and afterwards. It should not be possible for anyone reading a research report or other outputs to know who has taken part.

For children and young people, relevant personal data under the Data Protection Act 2018 will include their name, date of birth, national insurance number, child benefit number, address, pupil number and computer IP address. **Special category personal data** includes details about an individual's ethnicity, religion, health, disability and sexuality. Even if no names are used, a combination of details in a report can indirectly identify participants, such as the name or location of a school or group or specifying that someone has a disability.

Anonymity involves separating data from any personal identifiers, to make it impossible to link views or other data to an individual research participant or their family. Pseudo-anonymity requires developing keys to link personal identifiers and other data, storing the two types of data separately and securely, and taking additional measures to disguise the sources of quotes or case examples when reporting. For instance, if the report talks about a child from a particular background using a certain institution, it may be quite easy to identify them.

Privacy relates to a person's right to be protected from intrusion. There are arguably more privacy issues when working with children and young people: they may have less appreciation of privacy; be accustomed to adults overriding their privacy; often need assistance from gatekeepers and other adults to participate in research, and therefore their participation cannot be a private matter; and may be generally less assertive, or self-protective than adults. All research is intrusive to some degree. Here we take it to mean intruding into issues beyond the realms of the research and beyond what was formally consented to, for example their home composition or parents' work. It is best practice to avoid raising issues which are not directly pertinent, more-so if these are potentially sensitive.

EXAMPLE: RESPECTING PRIVACY

Research about the training, development and support needs of staff in children's homes included interviews with staff and young residents. The latter were asked about the skills, attributes, knowledge and approach they liked to see in staff. However, the questions were deliberately designed to avoid asking them anything about their background or why they were living in care.

EXAMPLE: RESPECTING PRIVACY

An evaluation of a support programme for young people who had been sexually exploited involved interviewing staff and young people to get their opinions on the new resources and any suggestions for improvement. Interview questions did not ask about the young people's experiences of sexual exploitation, but kept to views around the programme and resources. Professionals interviewed were reminded to avoid disclosing any young person's identity or personal history, and were instead asked to refer to them or the issue in very general terms.

Whose confidentially, anonymity and privacy?

When working with children and young people, it is their confidentiality, privacy and anonymity and that of their families, peers and friends which is of most concern. Others include those who were originally sampled but did not participate, and the wider population of institutions used by those researched, including school staff and pupils, youth clubs, or children in a residential home.

BOX 4.2: PRACTICAL DILEMMAS AND POTENTIAL STEPS TO HELP PROTECT CONFIDENTIALITY, PRIVACY AND ANONYMITY

- Information should state that participants will not be expected to talk about anything they don't want to.
- Stress that there is no expectation to talk about anything distressing.
- Where possible, spell out what types of private or confidential information will not be covered. For example, if exploring the views of a sub-group of children on say TV viewing, state that you will not need to talk about their family, if this is the case.

- Avoid straying off topic into private matters. For example, there is usually no reason to ask details about their family or friends, or health, or lifestyle, unless central to the research.
- If someone starts to share private details beyond the research topic, you may need to politely change the subject, and make it clear you are not recording those details.
- When using third parties, such as gatekeepers or interpreters, remind them about the principles of confidentiality and privacy. This can include: not giving the researchers details of the children who were sampled, but declined to participate; and only sharing essential details, such as first names, but not other personal details, such as date of birth, address, health or family circumstances, etc.
- Gatekeepers and others can sometimes expect the researcher to share confidential information with them. This needs to be politely refused.
- Some children and young people need close assistance from others to participate, for example help to communicate, or move. It is important to discuss confidentiality and privacy in advance and perhaps exclude certain topics if they are likely to be problematic.
- If relying on others to administer and collect questionnaires, include a mechanism to protect confidentiality and privacy. Advise the adults concerned to not ask the child about their answers, and not to look at what the children write; and provide envelopes for respondents' completed forms.
- If children or young people are completing surveys individually in a group setting, such as a classroom, ensure their answers cannot be seen by other respondents.
- Avoid situations where conversations can be overheard. Try to use neutral, private and confidential venues which are also easy to get to and from. Using the family home, a service used, or a school all impact on privacy and confidentiality, as others know who has taken part and may overhear what is said. However they may be unavoidable for various reasons.
- If running a group discussion, discuss confidentiality at the start. However, even if the group agrees to 'keep what's said in the room in the room', this is impossible to police or guarantee. Advise participants that you do not expect them to share confidential or private information but be prepared for this happening.
- Participants may disclose safeguarding or other legal issues (such as immigration law and criminal offences) around which there is a general reporting duty. Ideally, the risk of any disclosures should be explored when planning the research, along with potential actions.

- When reporting, double-check for identifying factors, such as location, gender, age or how someone speaks. If, for some reason it is considered essential to attribute an issue or a quote, pseudonyms might be the answer.
- If using photographs, film, videos, try to avoid including people who did not give consent.

Balancing safeguarding concerns with research confidentiality

The welfare and safety of children and young people overrides research interests. It is best practice to anticipate safeguarding during planning. As mentioned earlier, one aspect is ensuring the research does not introduce or increase risk. Another is dealing with safe-guarding disclosures. Most organisations which work with children, young people or vulnerable adults, have their own policies and procedures and work within the local safeguarding protocols, which include named responsible people to involve if necessary and the process for dealing with reports. Normally researchers agree to work within any host agency's procedures and processes, as well as their own. Occasionally, a fresh protocol to fit the research is required. The NSPCC provides guidance on writing good policies.[20]

If during the research a researcher becomes concerned about a child's or young person's safety or welfare, they are expected to follow the agreed procedure. Broadly speaking, this involves the following steps (but check your own organisation's procedure and that of any other agency involved):

- tell the child or young person that you are concerned about what they have brought up and that you think you may need to talk to someone else about it;
- usually ask the child or young person not to tell you any more right now (and don't question them further);

[20] www.nspcc.org.uk/preventing-abuse/safeguarding/writing-a-safeguarding-policy/

- ask if they have already informed any other professional about this matter;
- hand over the issue to the person responsible for safeguarding; and
- discuss the matter with your line manager and/or the safeguarding officer in your organisation, to help decide if any other actions needed and ensure appropriate action has been taken.

In anticipation of safeguarding issues emerging during the research, 'the normal promise to protect confidentiality has to be tempered'. In other words, written information and what is said at the start of any fieldwork regarding confidentiality carries a caveat, for instance: '... unless anything is said which makes me concerned about your safety or well-being, or someone else's safety or well-being'.

Social media research and confidentiality, privacy and anonymity

Using social media, for social research raises several privacy and confidentiality issues. Children and young people may be (even) less familiar than adults with their rights and what the terms and conditions they 'agreed' to originally actually cover. The Data Protection Act 2018 and associated guidance recognises their additional vulnerability and emphasises their rights, including, as they get older, to request disclosure of all personal data held on them and their rights to full erasure. Ethical questions also hinge on what might count as 'public' data and what permission, if any, users have given to have their data or views accessed or used by third parties, such as researchers. It may be especially difficult to report on findings from a social media source and simultaneously respect and protect members' anonymity, privacy and confidentiality.

Joining a private forum or 'chatroom' such as a mutual support group carries several risks. For instance, the researcher's presence might influence and bias the discussion; people may leave the forum if they have worries about confidentiality, privacy or anonymity; members may no longer talk openly, which undermines the forum's usefulness; and worst of all the forum may close down. On the other hand, if the researcher pretends to be just another member and researches covertly, that deception would usually be unsupportable ethically. Moreover, if found out, it could harm members' trust in such groups.

Young Digital[21] suggest that if too many ethical issues arise when attempting to use a type of digital media or internet-based tool, it may be best to consider a different method.

EXAMPLE: ONLINE RESEARCH AFFECTING GROUP DYNAMICS

A researcher with a personal and research interest in a disabling condition joined an online self-help forum which comprised other people with the same condition. The group did not have a strict membership system, or a formal moderator or convener. In other words, people joined in or not as they wished. The researcher wanted to observe the group and how it worked and get users' views on the benefits of having an online support group. The researcher told the other forum members this. Whether coincidentally or not, the group ceased to function after a while.

TOP TIPS: CONFIDENTIALITY

- Assess potential risks to confidentiality, anonymity and privacy during planning, as well as being alert to emerging issues, for example, in relation to sampling, methods, fieldwork location and so on.
- Discuss risks and mitigating actions with all fieldworkers.
- Ensure all researchers are up to date with data protection legislation and how it applies to children and young people and child protection.
- Be ready to remind others, not least gatekeepers and other professionals, about the need to protect confidentiality, anonymity and privacy.
- Ensure all fieldworkers are familiar with the relevant agencies' safeguarding procedures and how to apply these.
- The potential safeguarding exception to confidentiality needs to be explained (briefly) in information materials as well as during fieldwork.

---

[21] www.youngdigital.net/ethical/ethics-and-digital-media

Avoiding bias

The most common additional risks of bias when working with children and young people arise during recruitment and fieldwork.

Potential bias which can emerge in recruitment and sampling

- Some groups of children and young people are *less visible* and known and therefore unwittingly excluded from sampling frames. Migrant children, children who do not attend mainstream education and emerging subcultures are just some examples.
- On the other hand, some groups may end up being inadvertently *over-researched*, as they are more visible or vocal (such as a local participation group), or easier to target and sample (including school pupils).
- As *intermediaries and gatekeepers* are more necessary when recruiting children and young people to research (than when working with adults), their own biases often influence sampling. For example, they might think it is best to recruit more articulate children who are more likely to voice opinions, or they may choose the 'nicer' and more 'cooperative' children. Conversely, in schools, pupils may be chosen for convenience, or because they have space in their timetable. To put this another way, to ensure a wide sample, can take more time and perseverance.
- *Budget and time* restraints often militate against reaching those less often heard, not least disabled children and young people, those with literacy issues, pupils excluded or missing from school and those who are less familiar with or confident about research.
- Using an opt-out system with *parents and guardians* may create a bias towards adults who are less intimidated by research, or are themselves more opinionated, and those who have better literacy in English.

Potential bias during fieldwork includes:

- If the questions go outside a child's capacity, experience and memory there is a risk that they feel they need to give any answer, rather than say they don't know.
- Unclear *language* and questions create a barrier for those who are less literate, or who have less time to read information or complete a survey. Matching the child's language skills is important in written and verbal communication.
- Because of *power* dynamics, children and young people may try to anticipate the 'right answer', 'please' researchers, follow their peers, or give the answer they heard their parents or other influential people give. Careful design, using a mixed methodology and a range of tools and questions covering the same topic, can all help reassure young participants that it is '*their*' view you want and that there is no 'right answer'.

EXAMPLES: SAMPLING BIAS

A research study was undertaken with young people aged 12 to 16, using focus groups. Schools helped recruit young people. In one school the staff had selected certain pupils because they were the most likely to have views on this topic, and known to be the most articulate. In another, the researchers were given the pupils who had been excluded from all the other classes because of their behaviour. They were not happy and had no interest in the research. Most of the scheduled time was taken up with trying to get their interest.

TOP TIPS: BIAS

- Assess potential risks of bias during planning, and be alert to others emerging later.
- Provide scripts for intermediaries who are assisting with recruitment.
- Develop methods, tools and questions carefully and pilot these with appropriate age-groups and discuss with all fieldworkers.

• A mixed-methods approach helps reduce the impact of any bias associated with any individual method.

KEY POINTS

• There is an additional onus on researchers to try even harder to get ethics 'right' when working with children and young people because of their additional vulnerability, diversity and relative lack of research experience.
• The issues and challenges are highlighted to help prepare the researcher, not put you off doing research.
• The ethical aspects are closely interrelated and overlapping. Many balances to be struck, for example ensuring children and young people exercise their rights to have their experiences and perspectives researched, while both protecting them from harm and helping them benefit from the research.
• A risk assessment helps anticipate and plan for the issues most likely to arise.
• Informed consent is fundamental and extra care may be needed to ensure that information is accessible and understood.
• Layering information, getting input and advice from children, young people and suitably qualified organisations all helps maximise accessibility.
• Given power dynamics and lack of familiarity with research, consent is best approached as an incremental and continuous process.
• Responsiveness and close observation, to check understanding and any indirect withdrawal of consent are vital.
• Although gatekeepers are usually involved to mediate contact and help seek consent from children and young people under 16, (and help protect their interests) nothing removes the child's or young person's autonomous right to consent, or not, themselves.
• Researchers need to be even more proactive to protect children's and young people's confidentiality, privacy and anonymity.
• Many are unaware of immediate or long-term risks and are often accustomed to others sharing their data.
• However if safeguarding concerns emerge, the researcher may have to breach confidentiality.
• Bias easily emerges in sampling and recruitment, especially if gatekeepers presume you want to talk to the most articulate children, or the easiest to reach. Young participants may presume you want certain/ more desirable answers.

- Once issues are recognised, solutions will be found and many are suggested above. In other words, ethics alone should not be used as an excuse for avoiding doing research with children and young people. Anticipation, careful planning, accessible design and considering alternatives usually provide the answers.

References

Alderson, P. and Morrow, V. (2011) *The Ethics of Research with Children and Young People. A practical handbook*. London: Sage

British Psychological Society (2017) *Ethics Guidelines for Internet-mediated Research*. Available from: www.bps.org.uk/news-and-policy/ethics-guidelines-internet-mediated-research-2017

Department of Health (2010) *Making Written Information Easier to Understand for People with Learning Disabilities: Guidance for People Who Commission or Produce Easy Read Information*, revised edn. London: Department of Health

Dingwall, R., Iphofen, R., Lewis, J., Oates, J., with Emmerich, N. (2014) *Towards Common Principles for Social Science Research Ethics: A Discussion Document for the Academy of Social Sciences Academy of Social Sciences Working Group*, Version 2. London: Academy of Social Sciences. Available from: www.acss.org.uk/developing-generic-ethics-principles-social-science/previous-activities/jan-2014-conference-british-library/

General Medical Council (2018) *0–18 years, Good Medical Practice: Guidance for All Doctors on Assessing Capacity to Consent*. London: GMC. Available from: www.gmc-uk.org/ethical-guidance/ethical-guidance-for-doctors/0-18-years/making-decisions

Graham, J., Grewal, I. and Lewis, J. (2007) *Ethics in Social Research: the views of research participants*. London: GSRU

GSRU (2011) *Ethical Assurance for Social Research in Government*. London: Government Social Research Unit. Available from: www.gov.uk/government/publications/ethical-assurance-guidance-for-social-research-in-government

GSRU Social Media Research Group (2016) *Using Social Media for Social Research: An Introduction*. London: Government Social Research Unit. Available from: www.gov.uk/government/publications/social-media-research-guidance-using-social-media-for-social-research

INVOLVE, National Institute for Health Research (2018) *Payment and Recognition for Public Involvement*. Southampton: INVOLVE. Available from: www.invo.org.uk/resource-centre/payment-and-recognition-for-public-involvement/

Market Research Society (MRS) (2012) *Guidelines for Online Research*. London: Market Research Society. Available from: www.mrs.org.uk/pdf/2012-02-16%20Online%20Research%20Guidelines.pdf

Morrow, V. (2009) *The Ethics of Social Research with Children and Families: Practical Experiences*, Working Paper 53. Oxford: Young Lives, Dept of International Development, University of Oxford. Available from: www.younglives.org.uk/sites/www.younglives.org.uk/files/YL-WP53-Morrow-EthicsOfResearchWithChildren.pdf

5
DESIGNING APPROPRIATE METHODS FOR CHILDREN AND YOUNG PEOPLE

Introduction

This chapter provides an overview of key issues and considerations in designing robust methodologies, methods, indicators and tools for children and young people. Poorly considered methods and questions, which includes those which do not match diverse circumstances and needs, can result in low response rates, biased answers and poor data. Methods, tools and questions which work well with adults need careful reconsideration and adaptation to suit children and young people.

It is not possible to cover every research permutation, but the principles suggested should help build a framework applicable to most studies. This chapter focuses on common primary qualitative and quantitative methodologies. Literature reviews and the secondary use of administrative, social media or other big data are not discussed as there does not seem to be a particular children's or young people's angle to the methods per se.

The chapter aims to address issues and practical solutions which most generalist publications omit. Do not be daunted: to be comprehensive it needs to cover a range of research circumstances, but not all apply in each research study. Moreover, the chapter provides plenty of suggestions, along with examples, drawn from the authors' extensive experience. A key bedrock is inclusivity and careful planning. After looking overarching at design principles, including diversity, accessibility, sensitive topics and practical factors, this chapter looks at the specific considerations in adapting common quantitative and qualitative approaches and developing creative methods. Rather than attempting to provide an exhaustive set of instructions, or examples for every potential permutation (which is probably impossible), the emphasis here is on providing general parameters to ensure methods are appropriate and accessible.

Planning methods and questions to match the diversity of children and young people

As discussed in previous chapters, although 'children and young people' is a widely used term, they are a far from homogeneous group. Researchers need to consider all children and young people, and/or the particularities of a precise target group when determining the best methodology. Taking an inclusive approach involves looking beyond collecting data from the easiest to reach, including the voices of those less frequently heard and avoiding over-researching some sub-groups. From the outset, it is best to presume that you will be working with numerous, if overlapping groups, who share some commonalities (typically age).

Children's and young people's life experiences and views, as well as their ability to interact effectively with different research methods will vary according to numerous factors, including age, ethnicity, culture, disability, gender, socioeconomic situation and living circumstances, as well as their cognitive and emotional development. The main aspects of diversity which need to be borne in mind when designing methodologies, tools and questions are grouped as follows:

- backgrounds, circumstances and life experiences, including culture, ethnicity, family composition and income;
- cognitive development, concentration, memory and energy;
- ensuring accessibility;
- covering sensitive topics adn being reflexive; and
- practical factors, including location and timing.

Recognising diverse backgrounds, family circumstances and life experience

Children and young people are largely dependent on their families' and carers' circumstances and behaviour for their own life experiences. The family's income, social class, housing, religion, culture, education, health and disability impact on a child's and young person's development and experiential differences.

For instance, family composition is important when framing questions. A large proportion of children do not live in a two-parent household, or with either or both of their birth parents. Many have half- and/or step-siblings, and at any one time roughly 96,000 children in Britain are in care. Furthermore, many young people 'sofa-surf', live in hostels or other temporary accommodation, but do not usually appear in the looked after or homeless statistics. Family employment, income, health and housing range immensely. At the time of writing, roughly one in three UK children were classified as living in poverty,[1] which will be reflected in fewer material possessions, activities and experiential differences. In practical terms, this means it would be excluding and cause embarrassment if research questions presume that all children and young people live in a 'nuclear' family, have access to a computer or mobile phone, or have their own bedroom, or have had family holidays.

Anything that would normally be kept private, such as family income and social circumstances, would normally count as 'sensitive', even

---

[1] The figure was 30% in 2016/17 according to the 'households below average income' statistics; see www.gov.uk/government/statistics/households-below-average-income-199495-to-201617

if the child or young person is unaware of this. Extra consideration is needed when designing methods, tools and questions to avoid compromising confidentiality or triggering embarrassment, stigma, or bullying, for example, asking children where they last went on holiday, or about their father's or mother's work. Sensitive and special category data are covered in more detail below.

Diverse cognitive development, memory and understanding

As discussed in Chapter Two, all children and young people are experts in their own lives and have rights and agency in relation to research. That said, how and when children and young people are able to participate in research will vary in relation to their development and a variety of other factors. In other words, the way in which you would approach research with most 5-year-olds will be substantially different than with 10-year-olds, and different again for 17-year-olds. These differences partly relate to cognitive development and the expansion of memory, attention span, concentration, emotional maturation, self-awareness and the ability to objectify and think in the abstract. All of these contribute to the concept of 'competence' in research terms.

Although intellect, understanding and memory generally expand as a child gets older, as with consent, age is not the only yardstick for cognitive development, or for deciding appropriate methodology and methods. Within broad age generalisations, there are wide variations and each child is distinct. In other words, even if planning to work with one single age-group of similar needs, such as a school class, expect a range of abilities.

Varied capacity impacts on the topics a researcher can explore, the suitability of different tools, how to word questions and ultimately the scope for obtaining reliable data. For example, questions which require accuracy of memory or abstraction are not going to work with young children, or with those with some learning disabilities. A 6-year-old may know their current favourite game or food, but not accurately remember what they ate or did the previous week, let alone month. Therefore, a question which relies heavily on memory or theorising may produce unreliable results. On the other hand, most 14-year-olds could be asked how their tastes have varied over time, their activities over a previous period and what factors influence their preferences. In addition, many could be expected to hypothesise around social concepts and issues, such as healthy living initiatives, education policies or social justice.

Attention spans and concentration also vary by age and can be further affected by learning and other disabilities, mental health problems, tiredness, emotional upset, pain and other factors. For the researcher this means that a research session with a young child or someone who is distressed needs to be kept quite brief and ideally include a mix of activities. Conversely, expecting a child to maintain focus for extended periods of time may cause discomfort, undermine the ethical principal of avoiding harm and make the research tedious.

Language and literacy skills vary by age and can also be affected by certain disabilities or additional needs. To make your research appropriate for as many children and young people as possible, it will be critical to consider how to design methods, tools and questions to maximise accessibility. Rather than design endless versions, it is simplest to target written materials towards those with the lower literacy skills.

Sometimes younger or less confident children are more liable to be influenced by others (their peers, or key adults), or display more 'respondent bias' and give answers which they think the researcher wants. Mixing methods and tools helps to circumvent this risk. As they develop, children are more likely to appreciate autonomy and become more able and confident in voicing their individual views.

Ensuring accessibility

Ensuring full accessibility for every child and young person targeted is an essential challenge to overcome, if a full range of data is to be gathered. What precisely is needed will vary according to individuals' specific needs. Again, rather than creating endless versions of tools, which is costly and can undermine reliability, it normally suffices to create one design for each broad group, determined by needs, comprehension and literacy levels.

Methods and tools need to be clear so that the participants know what is being asked and can easily convey their views, experiences and so on. Keep methods, topics, tools, questions and language as straightforward as possible, and aim at those with more access needs in the sample, for example those with lower literacy abilities. It is best practice to discuss access needs with the children and young people in question and their parents, carers or key professionals, to explore what will work best to ensure they can participate meaningfully. This may include changing the format, style and delivery of methods and tools.

For example, children with sight impairments may prefer questions to be asked orally, or to use a computer, or to have printed materials magnified. For others, visual prompts can help. Some children and young people need assistance to write. Children and young people who use communication aids might be able to respond independently or need a parent or carer to interpret, or scribe for them. Some children simply need extra time, a quiet room, or a taxi to get to a research venue.

Draft survey instruments need to be tested with a representative group. Qualitative methods allow a certain amount of adaptation in situ (if the planning and testing was not enough on its own). For example, the wording of interview or focus group questions can be amended to suit the interviewee or group and respond to issues and circumstances arising. Ideally the range can be anticipated in advance and the phrasing agreed to maximise consistency, but researchers often have to think on their feet as needs become clearer.

A bespoke approach may be necessary for children and young people with highly complex needs, such as severe cognitive impairment, as exemplified in the example of the 'bespoke approach'. Guidance from parents, carers or key professionals will be essential in developing the core questions and how to ask these.

EXAMPLE: BESPOKE APPROACH

A disability organisation developed a new set of workshop and information materials to help children and young people understand their rights in relation to health services. The pilot materials were tested and evaluated to ensure they would work with a wide range of children and young people. One group of young people who tested the new materials had complex learning disabilities. Many used communication aids and relied on carers and staff to interpret.

After discussing the young people's needs with staff in this setting, the evaluation methods and questions were redesigned, as their views and input were highly important for assessing how well the workshops would work with others with learning disabilities.

As a result, the evaluator did not visit the centre to do interviews as this would not have worked, as they would not easily have understood the young people and the young people might have been discombobulated by a strange. Instead, the questions were posed by staff whom the young people already trusted and with whom they could communicate effectively. The questions were reduced to four key topics and worded to be as straightforward as possible. Because of the additional risk of bias, for example the young people or staff wanting to be positive, the staff were carefully briefed on how to present questions to minimise this.

The key factor in all of this is to expect diversity as the norm, and to be adaptable and responsive. It helps to ask for information about access or support needs when liaising with gatekeepers. If using any intermediaries, such as interpreters and signers, gently remind them that the research is primarily interested in what the child or young person wants to say and that you need their words verbatim. Involving children and young people in the research design process, and/or testing and piloting methods, indicators, tools and questions will help ensure these are more robust and reliable. Using a mixed methodology boosts accessibility as well as providing more robust data.

Covering sensitive topics

'Sensitive' data is a broad term. It includes what the Data Protection Act 2018 terms as 'special category data', such as gender, sexual orientation, genetics, ethnicity, health, disability and religious or political beliefs. But it is wider than that and arguably encompasses anything that people would normally keep private, such as income, family composition and circumstances, as well as individual vulnerabilities. Research around special category or sensitive topics should not be avoided because it is difficult, as it can be important to expand knowledge about these matters and gather the perspectives of those with first hand experience. Careful planning helps ensure these are covered appropriately and ethically. The additional dimensions when working with younger participants is the interface with ethical principles discussed in Chapter Four (for example, consent, confidentiality and privacy), and with cognition, maturity, awareness and self-confidence. Sensitive topics may be anticipated, or emerge spontaneously, for instance in a discussion about something apparently innocuous and unconnected.

If sensitive topics are central to the research and expanding understanding of an issue, the challenge is to devise the best methods, tools and questions to collect that data without compromising confidentiality, or triggering embarrassment, stigma or bullying.

Methods, tools or questions which have an indirect cultural, racial, gender, religious or sexuality bias may effectively exclude groups of children and young people. In contrast with adults, they may not have enough knowledge, experience, or confidence to tell you this.

- When selecting methods, Questionnaires offer more privacy and anonymity but may be inadequate for exploring matters in any depth. However it is easy for the young respondent to skip a question about a sensitive topic.
- As a general rule, group discussions are rarely suitable, as it is not always possible to anticipate (prevent) sensitive issues emerging; and it can be difficult to protect confidentiality and privacy or respond adequately to each individual, despite the best ground rules and promises. There is the added risk of generating discomfort, discrimination and bullying. These problems can be mitigated if the group has convened around the issue which is the subject of the research (such as a self-help group), members already know

each other and have agreed ground rules and/or there is a group convenor who can respond to issues afterward.

- Individualised settings, such as face-to-face depth interviews arguably provide the most scope for the researcher to explore and respond to sensitive issues and personal nuances and gauge the impact of discussing this topic and respond accordingly.

While it is best practice to anticipate potential sensitive issues which might emerge during fieldwork, they often arise spontaneously. If so, and as discussed in Chapter Four, there are ethical dimensions around deciding whether to continue. In general, if not directly germane to the research it is more ethical not to. For example, is there any need to discuss a distressing family situation, unless it is central to the research topic? Children and young people may not appreciate that they have raised a 'sensitive' topic, and the associated consequences and risks in the immediate and long term (not least from social media, gossip or bullying). In a group setting, try to avoid drawing undue attention to the individual and tactfully remind participants about maintaining confidentiality. It may be necessary to stop that line of conversation and offer to discuss the matter with the individual afterwards. Switching off any recording device and doing so in an obvious manner reinforces this point, as well as protecting confidentiality. Allowing a short break helps if someone gets upset, and also gives an opportunity to discuss what they prefer to do next.

Being responsive and flexible

The need to treat the research process as an evolving and dynamic interaction and to be responsive is even more imperative when working with children and young people. Even if pre-tested and piloted, methods need to be flexible enough for you to respond to what happens during the research process. This is easier with qualitative approaches. For example, the researcher needs to observe carefully how children or young people are responding to questions and behaving.

If a topic gets no response it might simply be that it does not fit their circumstances and a slight rewording would work better.

Being attentive to body language and non-verbal cues as well as what is voiced out loud helps in checking for ongoing consent; ensures that tools and questions are suitable; and informs any adaptation to timing or questions to make them better match abilities, concentration and energy levels.

Usually, the more relaxed the children or young people feel in the location, with the researchers and with the research, the more honest, open and interactive they will be. As discussed in Chapter Four, children and young people tend to be less assertive and confident than adults. Therefore body language, such as fidgeting or becoming monosyllabic, withdrawn or disruptive may be their indication that they want to change the subject or withdraw consent. Rather than persevering doggedly, plan some alternative methods, tools or questions in advance; and/or take a short break and then discuss how they would like to continue.

On top of the normal consent information, and conveying that participation is optional, specific points need more emphasis. For example, remind them that:

- answering each question is also a choice;
- the research is not a test and there are no right or wrong answers;
- everyone is an individual and that the diversity of individual viewpoints is important and what you are interested in: in other words you do not want them to simply repeat their friends' or family's views; and
- to tell you that they are getting tired or need a break.

Practical design factors when planning fieldwork

Practical considerations include fieldwork location, timing and other matters. Again, these overlap with ethical considerations covered in Chapter Four and a general good practice principle is to work closely with gatekeepers, children and young people to see what would work both for them and the research subject.

Location

The fieldwork site is important, as it can help or hinder children and young people to feel relaxed, comfortable and safe. Selecting a suitable location involves striking a balance across different practical, methodological and ethical considerations, not least personal safety and minimising disruption. Many children and young people are not accustomed, able or allowed to travel alone and it may not be safe for them to do so.

Children may be more at ease in a place they know well, such as school, or a familiar service building, or their home. It can also be more inclusive and accessible if the researcher travels to where the children and young people already are, rather than expecting them to travel.

On the other hand, using such venues can undermine privacy, confidentiality and openness. While using the child's home eliminates costs and travel-related risks, it can impinge on the whole family's privacy and confidentiality, as well as that of the child or young person, and is only feasible for one-to-one or family-based data collection (e.g. interviews). Completing a questionnaire at home, avoids travel. However, it can be difficult to ascertain whose views are being entered and if the child completed it independently or with input from parents or carers.

Time

The general dictum is to keep all methods, research sessions and activities short and sweet, and avoid over-tiring participants, which simultaneously ties in with the principle of minimising harm. This might require modifying expectations around how much can be covered in any one research encounter. Piloting helps.

When scheduling fieldwork children's and young people's multiple time commitments need to be respected. These can include education, homework, exam periods, after-school sport and other activities, caring obligations, religious observance, family commitments and work. Gatekeepers also have schedules and rhythms to fit around. Evening fieldwork avoids impinging on schools, college or work, but necessitates travelling at night. Weekends or school holidays may work better. In relevant cases, research can be done when participants are using a service, especially if this service is being evaluated. However, while avoiding additional travel or time commitment for participants it is harder for them to opt out and may not be suitable for sensitive topics.

TOP TIPS: GENERAL METHODOLOGICAL AND DESIGN ISSUES

- Co-design, pilot and test draft tools and questions with children and young people of the same age and ability. Ideally, conduct cognitive testing with a representative group.
- Keep tools and language as straightforward and accessible as possible.
- Avoid jargon, technical or research terms.
- Seek advice from the professionals or carers on the broad suitability of topics for a your sample, for example, ask their teacher or youth worker.
- As well as considering age, get specific advice on mental competence, accessibility and other considerations and any individual's additional needs.
- Many disability organisations provide advice about designing materials accessibly.
- Allow enough time for piloting, adapting and revising tools.
- Plan a range of activities to maintain momentum and interest, minimise the intensity and appeal to different preferences and help maintain enjoyment for participants.
- Chunk an overall session into different types of activities, tools and questions.
- Use creative methods (see next section).
- Time spent on introductions, 'breaking the ice' and helping young participants feel comfortable is time well spent.
- Keep the session and each activity as brief as possible, in recognition of variable concentration and focus.
- Allow enough time for children or young people to complete each research task.
- Be hyper-alert to tiredness or disengagement and plan alternate activities, and breaks.

- Be ready to be flexible and responsive and have adaptations up your sleeve.
- If the energy is flowing, follow that momentum (to a limit: breaks are still important).
- Plan suitable alternative activities in advance for children who do not want to take part or want to withdraw, which do not draw extra attention to them.

If covering sensitive topics:

- Plan methods and questions which minimise impact and fit the sensitivity of the topics.
- Repeat consent principles at the start of data collection and occasionally throughout.
- Allow for additional breaks and time out.
- In anticipation of someone getting upset, provide scope for the researcher, or another trusted adult to talk to them individually.
- Prepare written information and details of support agencies around this issue.
- Set up a support mechanism, such as a specific member of staff, or a specialist counsellor.
- Inform the gatekeeper, parent or support worker or other person who helped organise contact, if a child or young person gets upset, with the latter's permission.
- Follow safeguarding protocols (see Chapter Four).

Considerations around specific research methods

There are no special research methodologies or methods for data collection with children and young people. Rather, 'normal' research approaches must match the needs, abilities and other considerations regarding the children and young people in question. This section looks at the benefits and challenges of quantitative surveys, qualitative interviews and focus groups, case studies and creative methods, and suggests ways to mitigate common challenges.

Quantitative surveys

As with any age-group, surveys offer many advantages. They can provide greater anonymity and privacy, reach larger numbers relatively cheaply, can be administered in numerous ways, including paper, online, text or email and, if self-completed, respondents can do them when they please. Each administration method, whether paper, online, self-completion, or a face-to-face structured interview, has its discrete considerations regarding suitability for children and young people.

Self-completion questionnaires

Language and literacy are the primary hurdles for all self-completion modes. In other words, can the target group read and fully comprehend the questions and express themselves adequately in that language in writing?

Careful framing of questions and keeping all text brief and unambiguous helps, but at 'normal development rates', the National Children's Bureau (Shaw et al, 2011) advise against using a self-completion questionnaire with children under 12, unless they have support. Length and the time required impacts on response rates. In other words, questionnaires need to be quite short.

Self-completion questionnaires may be inaccessible for children who cannot read or write in that language and for those with dyslexia or serious cognitive impairment. Creating accessible versions may help to some extent, as can adding images and graphics, and providing individual assistance, but reliability then becomes a challenge.

Last but far from least, covering sensitive topics is more challenging: it is impossible to gauge how the child or young person is coping with these questions; and harder to provide reassurance or support.

Online surveys

Surveys to be completed on a website, an online platform, or sent via email, or text, have additional considerations.

- Some young respondents do not have reliable or private access to a computer, the internet, or a smartphone, or the skills to use them. This can skew response rates and representativeness, create risks to confidentiality and privacy, and possibly deny more vulnerable and deprived groups a voice.
- Ethical challenges are discussed in Chapter Four, not least the difficulties in ensuring informed consent, confidentiality or privacy; or verifying permission from gatekeepers for those under 16.
- It is impossible to ascertain how much the views expressed are those of the child or young peerson or the person helping them complete the survey, especially if they need help to write.

That said, many agencies successfully use online platforms and mobile phone apps to collect data from children and young people. One national youth agency gathers feedback about the effectiveness of its programmes from the young participants by sending two questions by text a few months after taking part. Answers are collated in a database. Consent had previously been established and the survey's brevity and simplicity works well.

If setting up online sites or fora the Market Research Society recommends that a clear link is provided to enable children and young people to report any bullying or inappropriate behaviour to the Child Exploitation and Online Protection Centre (CEOP).[2]

Face-to-face survey administration

This may offset the numerous challenges listed above. In addition, a face-to-face approach can include some self-completion elements to supplement the questions posed by the researcher, alongside other methods. A disadvantage shared with qualitative interviews, is the risk of respondent bias. In other words, the child or young person may try to anticipate and please the researcher and give 'desired' responses.

[2] www.mrs.org.uk/pdf/2012-02-16%20Online%20Research%20Guidelines. pdf, p 19

TOP TIPS: SURVEYS

- Keep survey instruments, and individual questions, short, clear and simple.
- Get advice from, and cognitively test survey instruments with children and young people of a similar ages and abilities.
- Pilot, pilot, pilot and pilot again with a suitably representative group.
- Ensure the overall time required is as short as possible to minimise fatigue and attrition.
- Include a variety of questions.
- Include some open questions, to allow for individual and anticipated variations.
- If an 'online' survey by computer or text message or mobile app is the best method, try to think of ways to address the challenges listed earlier in this section.
- Use other methods (or example, qualitative ones) alongside the survey to get more depth and investigate the parameters of responses, especially around sensitive topics.
- Provide scope for respondents to give their reflections on the process.
- If sensitive topics may emerge, provide suggestions of where the respondent can get further information and/or support.

Qualitative depth interviews

This method has many advantages for this age-group as it:

- allows researchers to explain the research more thoroughly and ensure it is understood, provide reassurance, put the child or young person at ease, adapt the timing and delivery and ensure and check that they understand what is being asked;
- enables those being researched to frame their own concepts and priorities, and use their preferred language and means of expression;
- can be better for exploring subjective issues, experiences and views;
- enables the researcher to respond appropriately to the child's and young person's interests, abilities and other points emerging;

- is often better for covering sensitive topics, as the researcher is more able to broach the subject tentatively, judge discomfort and adjust the pace, wording, language, style as necessary;
- provides flexibility to clarify and reframe questions in more accessible ways to suit individual children and young people;
- helps bring new and unanticipated issues to light and explore wider and unrecorded dimensions of topics.

On the down side, a one-to one setting can be very intense for a child or young person. Many are unused to a straight question and answer session and find it intimidating and inhibiting, particularly with an adult (stranger). The power dynamic is very evident and there is arguably a greater risk that the personal dynamic inadvertently encourages a tendency to give 'desirable' answers to please the researcher, in other words, creates a bias. It can also be necessary for a parent or a carer to be present in the case of a young child to ensure their safety and protection, or to assist a child or young person who has additional needs, for example to communicate. Their presence, even if essential, may influence what the child says.

TOP TIPS: QUALITATIVE INTERVIEWS

- Start with an easy ice-breaker topic, game or creative method and easy, age-appropriate, questions about themselves (without getting too personal).
- Plan a range of different activities and tools and ensure the session is not all questions and answers.
- Have alternatives at hand to cover the same topic. If something does not work, drop it, and use another option.
- To reduce intensity, avoid sitting face-to-face. Sit a bit to the side and do some activities in parallel with the child.
- Offering a paired interview, for instance with a friend, can reduce intensity.
- Discussing hypothetical situations or vignettes, using a character of a similar age and background can make it easier to discuss sensitive topics, and helps protect confidentiality and privacy.
- Demonstrate 'active listening': taking notes all the time is offputting.

- If a parent or carer needs to be present, remind them that it is the child's or young person's input you need.
- If assistance is needed, such as with communication, it is best to brief the carer in advance about what the questions will cover and the need to enable and convey the child's own views and words as much as possible.

Focus groups

A group discussion can be easier for some children and young people, as they may feel safer and more relaxed with their peers. The group dynamic and interaction can help elicit rich data, as they bounce ideas off and react to each other and the ideas circulating. Moreover, the researcher can probe the breadth and depth of different viewpoints.

Group dynamics, such as gender and confidence, can influence how people behave and contribute in a focus group. Pre-existing groups, such as a classroom, are likely to already contain friendship circles, cliques and other power relationships, including bullying. These are likely to be unknown to the researcher but will affect group processes and the ensuing data. Group dynamics will also emerge in groups convened solely for the research: from the start some members will be more, or less, assertive, vocal, domineering or quiet.

Sensitive topics are a major consideration if using a group discussion, whether the topic is planned or emerges spontaneously. As mentioned previously, ensuring confidentiality is a major challenge. Most groups commence with a set of ground rules, including to respect the confidentiality of others. But is it feasible, desirable or ethical to ask children and young people to keep secrets? It might be better to advise participants to not raise any private matters, but some children and young people may not be aware that what they are talking about is sensitive information or the potential negative consequences. If something is raised, one option is to offer to discuss it individually with them afterwards (without drawing too much attention to this).

TOP TIPS: FOCUS GROUPS

- Plan a range of activities to maintain interest, suit different interests and abilities, and enable each person to express themselves in their own way.
- If visiting an existing group, get advice about the best ways to divide the group to balance power dynamics, including which people to place, or avoid placing, together.
- If working with a specially convened group, spend more time at the start on ice-breakers and developing healthy group cohesion.
- Subdivide the group in different combinations over the course of the session, to vary the group dynamics.
- Have tactics ready if one or two people tend to dominate the conversation or others stay quiet. Ideas include formal turn taking, varying sub-groupings, deliberately targeting the quieter ones (without intimidating them), introducing time limits for responses and deliberately using eye contact.
- Use hypothetical situations, vignettes or a character of a similar age and background to discuss sensitive topics, while protecting confidentiality and privacy.
- Available guidance on convening groups, for other purposes, for example youth groups, training is instructive on running research groups too.

Case studies

Here we define case study research as the detailed and intensive study of certain phenomena, using multiple data collection methods and a multiplicity of perspectives. The focus of a case study can be an individual child or young person, a family, or a service or programme, a geographical area, or a professional practice. Case studies can help explore and explain phenomena in depth and in various dimensions, in their natural environment, and produce very rich data. The advantages in relation to children and young people include the scope to establish trust with all parties over time and being able to conduct the study in the child's natural context; explore issues in depth and over time; use a range of methods; and triangulate data, which in turn may boost the reliability of the findings and be both multidimensional and individualised.

Additional challenges in relation to children and young people include minimising potential researcher influence and bias on findings; limiting the time commitment for children and families; and controlling for other variables, including natural maturation and other inputs.

TOP TIPS: CASE STUDIES

- Discuss in advance how to minimise the time and other commitment necessary from children, young people, families and others.
- Provide regular reminders to those participating that the research needs them to be as natural as possible and to try to ignore the researcher.
- Combine with other data sources to help offset other causative variables.

Creative methods

What are 'creative methods'?

The term 'creative methods' has several different interpretations. In the absence of a universally accepted definition, it will be an important first step to agree a shared definition across all the practitioners involved in the respective research project. Creativity extends to seeing the whole research plan from inception to dissemination creatively, which in turn might include greater involvement or co-production for those normally the subjects of the research (see Chapter Two). The term can also include research using technology and other 'transformative research frameworks' (Kara, 2015, p 3).

Here creative methods are not presented as a stand-alone genre, but rather as a general approach which can help make other common quantitative and qualitative methods (such as surveys, interviews and focus groups) more 'creative'. A major principle and benefit is that they are interactive, participatory, fun and open-ended. Just about any game or art form is adaptable to a research purpose and many are cheap and accessible.

The advantages of creative methods are that they:
- maximise interactivity and engagement;
- introduce a range of activities to maintain interest, momentum and concentration;
- reduce the 'them and us' barriers and help democratise the research interaction;
- reduce the pressure and intensity, enabling children and young people to feel more at ease, less like research 'subjects' and have some fun and enjoyment;
- circumvent reliance on the spoken or written word, being literate or verbally articulate;
- enable each person to express themselves in their own way, especially in a group setting;
- help participants relax and enjoy the activity. Most UK children and young people are quite familiar with playing and making art (possibly more so than adults);
- help free up thinking processes and help convey respondents' own agenda, issues and priorities and themes which otherwise are unknown to the researcher;
- augment and enrich data collection; and
- highlight additional avenues worth exploring.

However keep the following in mind as well:
- There may be a temptation to start with the creative method, such as making a film, rather than starting with the research aims and then determining the best method(s) to suit these (which might not include a creative method).
- Developing creative methods can take more time, especially in design and development.
- Some can be costly. Felt-tip pens and paper are cheap, but making a reasonable quality video, computer app or game can involve

hiring cameras, editing suites, professional training and guidance, and possibly fees for professionals and venues.

• Data protection, including storage, access and use around outputs such as films need consideration.

Figure 5.1: Tree

Source: Authors

Designing and developing creative methods for a research project

Developing creative methods can become another aspect of the researcher's essential toolkit. As may be evident from the suggestions given in Table 5.1, most common games and art techniques can be adapted relatively easily, but do not be limited to that list: think creatively. Like any method, creative tools must *match age, abilities and interests* and be *accessible and inclusive*: playing with puppets might be more suited to younger children, while writing a song or poem is likely to appeal more to an older group. *Time and budget* are major parameters. A video is a great reporting output and an effective way to illustrate personal experiences, but requires skills, equipment and training and thus a budget, as would support from an artist to create a mural, or a dramatist to teach acting skills.

The creative activity can be used to assist *group dynamics, as an ice-breaker, as a data collection tool or as a parallel activity*. For instance, while the child or young person is focused on drawing, the researcher can ask questions which may be related to the picture or not. Familiar group, ball and table-top games can help alter the momentum and energy in the research session. For example, a ball can be thrown (gently) around the group so that each catcher has to give a view on something, and so ensure that everyone gets a say. This is less intense and more enjoyable than more formal ways to take turns.

Creative tools can be used in both individual and group settings and gather *both quantitative and qualitative data*. For example, mystery shopping, inspection, diaries, post-its lend themselves to either methodology.

Quantitatively, stickers and post-its can be useful alternatives to voting, ticking options, or ranking responses to a question. These can be used in individual or group situations. Options can be presented in attractive ways, such as large images or wall charts and participants invited to vote on, or prioritise, their choices.

In a group, children can use themselves as 'counters', to vote. In the 'washing line' approach participants are invited to position themselves along a line in response to a statement or question posed by the researcher. Standing at one end of the line is designated to mean they *'totally agree'* (with that statement); the opposite end means they *'totally disagree'*; and points along the line reflect their level of agreement. The fruit bowl or musical chairs is a variation on this: participants move around if they fit certain criteria or agree with a given statement. These are both quick and light-hearted ways to get a rough idea of the range of views in a room, as well as to vary the momentum and group dynamics. Brief discussions can be facilitated if desired. A few light-hearted questions, unrelated to the main topic, such as what is their favourite ice cream flavour, help people relax.

As a *qualitative* method, adding a creative component can deepen and broaden understanding of topics from the point of view of those being researched, as this can provide more scope for the child or young person to initiate and define issues and parameters. Mapping, the river of life, photography, drama and so on all lend themselves to qualitative exploration. A group can be asked to draw what makes an 'ideal' practitioner. They start by drawing an outline of a person (use the researcher as the template), and then add in the ideal traits. These can include practical skills or actions (hands), understanding (head) and temperament or emotions (heart). These can be added individually or in a group. The associated discussion can include positive and negative examples in their own lives, and their reactions to these.

Reliably interpreting and analysing data from creative methods

To maximise reliability, questions need to be consistent, but the context in which they are posed alters. For instance, a child can be invited to talk about their family while they draw family members or share photographs, but the questions posed remain the same.

Similarly, most researchers are not likely to be trained as art therapists or have specialist expertise in interpreting paintings or other art. Unless you do, it is more robust to use creative methods as part of a broader data collection framework and to simply use and analyse the quantitative or qualitative data generated. For example, as the child is drawing and the researcher is asking questions, it is what the child says,

Figure 5.2: Post-it wall

Source: Authors

or how they recount their reality and interpretation of their creation which is the 'data', not the picture per se. That said, the latter might prompt some additional probes, for example, why is the child sad, how do they feel about that aspect, or why do they prefer to play in a particular place.

Table 5.1: Suggestions of potential creative methods

Method	Use and examples
Stickers	This is a quick way to get views on ranking and priorities. Doing it quickly helps anonymity. Using a bull's-eye graphic, pyramid, or similar hierarchical template helps 'score' an issue and quickly assess the range of opinions.
Post-its	These can be used to vote and rank as well as elicit individual ideas and parameters about a given topic. These can then be group and used as the starting point for discussions (see Figure 5.2).
Graffiti walls and murals	These can remain with the group and can be visually very appealing. Having an artist helps, but is not essential if the design is kept simple.
Emotion symbols / cards	These can be used as quick non-verbal ways to get a reaction to certain topics. Use sparingly.
Ranking	Pre-prepared cards with individual statements can be easier than asking people to talk on a topic from scratch. This has been used with young people to rank what activities they prefer, or what qualities they value in professionals who work with them.
Drawing and painting	Unless you are specifically trained, the idea is not to interpret the artwork as such, but to use it to generate discussion. Children and young people often find it easier to discuss issues while absorbed in the drawing or painting.
Collage and scrapbooks	This can be used in different ways, to generate discussion about a topic, and like diaries can be done as 'homework' (see Figure 5.5).

Method	Use and examples
Plasticine, sculpture, Lego	Like other art activities, the art process can be a parallel activity (for example, respondents making their favourite animal) while the discussion is going on; or the child or young person can be asked to create something relevant to inform that discussion. A 3-D model can be moved and altered, which might suit the topic better than a drawing.
Drama, music, poetry, song-writing	These probably require guidance from a music/ drama specialist. But in one project young people were asked to write a poem or song about the topic by the (lay) researcher and the young people enjoyed the task.
Props such as puppets or dolls	There is a long history of using these in development and health work. For example, the child can speak through the prop and act out a situation.
Photographs	These can be used in many different ways. In 'Photo-voice' a range of photographs are laid out. Each participant is encouraged to select one without too much thought, but then explain what that photograph means to them in relation to a given topic.
Photography or filming	This can help gather the child's or young person's perspectives on their environment. In one case, small children took pictures of the equipment they liked in a playground; in another, young people took photos of areas they perceived as dangerous or threatening in their neighbourhood. Arguably this is quite accessible as phones or disposable cameras can be used.
Mapping	This can be done in different ways. Geographically, children and young people can map a space or area they use, highlighting the locations of greatest importance, or focus on a theme (such as where bullying is most likely to happen, or which area is safest, or which they like most and why). Social dynamics and relationships and can also be mapped as a graphic. This serves as a helpful springboard for further exploration and the 'maps' produced are interesting visual representations.

Method	Use and examples
River of life	This is effectively another map, but with a longitudinal time element. It is a useful to examine processes, events, reactions and impact over time, on an individual or group basis. An example is provided in Figure 5.4. Drawing the 'river' and critical moments helps elicit and discuss participants' own or others' responses to key events, and views on the desired input from professionals or services. A large roll of paper and pens is all that is needed.
'Tree of life'	This is another way of pictorially gathering data on different processes. In one discussion group participants were asked to write their ideas onto post-its and stick these to the tree: the roots signified why people had joined this group; the tree-trunk the training and support received; the branches what they did in the programme; and the leaves and flowers any outcomes they had experienced. A cloud was added for future aspirations. See Figures 5.1 and 5.3.
Storyboards and vignettes	These can help elicit rich personal narratives and insights, while minimising exposure or embarrassment, as discussion focuses on fictional characters. This opens up the discourse while simultaneously protecting confidentiality and privacy. The researcher designs the starting point to match the topic, children or young people, and they fill in the rest of the story, including perhaps an 'ideal' outcome, and/or what professionals or others could do to help. Topical characters, from for example a TV soap opera are useful.
Mystery shopping and young inspectors	Children and young people enjoy judging services, possibly as it re-balances normal power dynamics. Training is needed and the audit criteria need to be agreed in advance. This can be a quantitative and/or qualitative assessment. Local participation groups, the NCB and the Council for Disabled Children have trained and used young inspectors.[3]

[3] www.probonoeconomics.com/sites/default/files/files/NCB%20report%20final.pdf; https://councilfordisabledchildren.org.uk/sites/default/files/field/attachemnt/Portsmouth%20case%20study%20UPDATED.pdf

Method	Use and examples
Diaries	Whether structured or semi-structured, diaries can help maintain momentum between research sessions, as 'homework'. They help collect rich and (more) accurate data about behaviour over time (in comparison to memory), for example on diet and exercise. A group investigating sex education collated images about, and recorded their responses to, media representations of women. If to be completed independently, this probably suits those over 11 most. But it can also work with families.
Jigsaws	These can schematically bring together the different aspects of an issue and open discussion about individual aspects of a given phenomenon as well as the whole. The pieces can be pre-determined or created by the participants.
Common table-top games, such as snakes and ladders, bingo, lotto, Jenga and card games	These can all be readily adapted. For instance, snakes and ladders can be useful to elicit examples of positive and negative incidents in a child's life, or in using a service. In snap or lotto special cards can be designed and discussion can be prompted when a person gets a match. 'Human bingo' helps people get to know each other and/ or can provide useful personal details.
Active group games and team exercises, such as with balls	Physical games and team activities can serve as ice-breakers and energise or calm down a group. A simple ball game can help introductions; or when each person catches the ball they have to say something about a topic. A parachute game or team drawing relay can be fun and help collect views.
An interactive computer game	This is likely to be much more expensive than any of the suggestions above. However, creating a game could be useful in gauging participants' reactions, behaviour and choices in different situations, especially if the sample is large and geographically spread out.

Figure 5.3: Tree of life

Source: Authors

EXAMPLE: 'RIVER OF LIFE'

A group of young people who all had a long-term illness were brought together to discuss how services could be improved for others with the same condition. A timeline was drawn (as a river) on a very long roll of paper (about 6m). The group decided the starting point, in terms of age and events. Prompts and questions helped fill in various details from then to the current day and into the future.

The 'journey' approach helped keep the discussion open to all, so that each young person could add their own story and emotions, as much as they wanted. It enabled a graphic representation of key 'stages' and events from

Figure 5.4: River of life

Source: Authors

different dimensions, including time, impact, their emotional reactions and the responses of key people. Members of the group shared writing onto the sheet. By the end of the session, the paper was full and clear. Seeing it all together prompted a further discussion and reflections about the process of this activity (see Figure 5.4).

EXAMPLE: SCRAPBOOK

A group of young people were co-producing new resources around sexual education to be used with children and young people to help reduce sexual exploitation. Between sessions they were asked to collate scrapbooks on different topics. One was on media representation of female and male bodies, including the photo-shopping of images of famous people, and the likely influence this would have on young people (see Figure 5.5).

TOP TIPS: CREATIVE METHODS

- Think creatively when developing creative methods.
- Explore how to integrate them in all projects.
- Look at common games, TV shows and art activities and see if any can be adapted.
- Ideally, co-produce these in partnership with children or young people of the same age, abilities and interests as those being researched.
- Always test and pilot, for suitability as well as time and types of data emerging.
- If something does not work, drop it and move on.
- Remember, unless the researcher is a trained art therapist, it is mainly the associated discussion which is of interest. So think about how best to record this.
- Don't let the tail wag the dog: keep in mind the overall research purpose and questions, as well as the budget and time.

Figure 5.5: Scrap book and collage

Source: Authors

KEY POINTS

- There are many methodological considerations to balance when planning research or evaluation with children and young people, which require much more than adding large fonts, current slang or smiley faces.
- The principles outlined here are not intended as a methods encyclopaedia, but rather as a framework within which researchers can build an appropriate methodology and suite of methods and tools.

- There is no discrete, or exclusively specialist, methodology for children and young people: researchers normally adapt methods from the common repertoire to match both the study and target group.
- As children and young people are not one homogeneous group, regardless of the precise study involved, it is essential to consider how to incorporate diverse needs and circumstances into the design.
- In addition to encompassing diversity around demographics, backgrounds and family circumstances, the methodology needs to match different abilities and needs.
- Sometimes a fresh perspective is required. Involving children and young people in the process can be invaluable in shaping topics, indicators, methods and tools.
- Although children and young people are typically grouped by age and broad developmental milestones, this is a very blunt tool and not reliable enough on its own for research purposes. Children and young people develop skills and abilities at their own speed.
- Methods, tools, indicators and questions need to take account of several highly individualised factors, not least cognitive development, memory, life experience, language and literacy skills.
- All these impact on the accessibility of a given method or tool and scope to reliably answer questions. Broadly speaking, tools reliant on literacy, such as questionnaires, will not suit young children.
- It is good practice to seek advice from those who know the children and young people in question to get input into design parameters. Advice is also needed around any additional access needs. Specialist disability and other organisations can advise on making communications and any written outputs as accessible as possible.
- Testing and piloting indicators and tools with children or young people who reflect the target group helps identify any changes needed.
- Practical factors are also critical, not least the location and timing of fieldwork, and allowing adequate time for each activity. Fieldwork needs to fit around children's and young people's often busy timetables; and all interactions and methods need to be brief.
- Reflection, adaptability and responsiveness are paramount throughout.
- Covering sensitive topics with children and young people overlaps with ethical principles, not least confidentiality, anonymity and privacy, as well as with the power dynamic in relation to adults.
- Researchers need to be observant during fieldwork, anticipate potential sensitive issues emerging and be prepared and responsive when they do.
- Arguably, extra care is required as children and young people may not realise the sensitivity of a topic, or that they are entitled to keep things

to themselves, or the long-term risk to their confidentiality, for example if such topics emerge in a group discussion.

- As well as the general principles, the chapter provides specific guidance around designing typical methods, including questionnaires, qualitative interviews and focus groups, as well as on developing creative methods.

- Working with children and young people allows great scope for using creative methods, as they are perhaps more willing to be openly creative than adults.

- Including some creativity reduces the intensity and any 'them and us' tension in a fieldwork situation. Besides tying in with the ethical principles of preventing harm and ensuring participation is enjoyable, this also produces better data.

- Arguably, creativity underpins all work with children and young people as the researcher needs to be imaginative and creative when designing robust and reliable methodology to meet all the diverse needs and considerations involved.

References

Kara, H. (2015) *Creative Research Methods in the Social Sciences: A Practical Guide*. Bristol: Policy Press.

Shaw, C., Brady, L.M. and Davey, C. (2011) *Guidelines for Research with Children and Young People*. London: National Children's Bureau. Available from: www.ncb.org.uk/resources-publications/resources/guidelines-research-children-and-young-people

6
CONCLUSIONS

This book makes the case for doing social research and evaluation about and with children and young people, and the key ethical and methodological considerations for doing so in ways that are meaningful, effective and inclusive. Our work as researchers and trainers has led us to believe that social research and evaluation with children and young people should, first and foremost, start with an understanding of children's and young people's rights to have a say in matters that affect them, not least as they are experts in their own lives. Good research and evaluation needs to be carried out in ways that enable children and young people to be listened to, so that the policies and services which they inform better reflect children's and young people's priorities and concerns. Their lived experience and agency should be valued and respected. Adult views may need to be considered as well as, but not as a proxy for those of the children they parent, teach or provide services for. In order to ensure that children's and young people's priorities and concerns are accurately reflected, it is critical to consider the diversity of children and young people both in general terms and in ensuring appropriate sampling and methods.

However, the theory and principles outlined in Chapters One and Two can be far from straightforward to put into practice, and we hope that the suggestions and examples in Chapters Three to Five help to provide ideas on how to apply the theory and principles outlined in Chapters One and Two in real research situations. At a time of limited budgets and, often, a need for fast results from social research and evaluation, there is often a considerable distance between the research we would like to do and the research we are able to do. As practising researchers, we are very aware of the constraints, but nonetheless argue that there is plenty of scope to ensure that the voices of children and young people are captured in ways that are ethically and methodologically sound.

Ethics is of course a key consideration in all social research and evaluation. And, as discussed in Chapter Four, there is an additional onus on researchers to try even harder to get ethics 'right' when working with children and young people, not least because of their additional vulnerability, diversity and relative lack of research experience. Ethical aspects are closely intertwined, and many balances need to be struck to meet the overarching principles of ensuring children and young people exercise their rights to be heard, while both protecting them from harm and providing benefit.

Because of power differentials and participants' relative inexperience of research, the researcher may need to be more pro-active, for example paying attention to the accessible design of information to ensure informed consent; devising ways to protect children's and young people's confidentiality, privacy and anonymity; and minimising bias in sampling, which easily arises if certain groups are over- or under-researched. However, in our experience, once issues are recognised solutions can be found. In other words, ethical concerns alone are rarely a valid reason for avoiding doing research with children and young people.

The fact that children and young people are not one homogeneous group is stressed throughout this book. Creating information, methods, tools, indicators and questions to match the diversity of children and young people requires more than changing font sizes or adding graphics. Poorly considered methods result in poor data. We have found that children and young people respond positively to well-considered methods; when researchers are reflexive, inclusive and responsive; and to being included in the design processes. Piloting and testing helps to ensure that methods and questions are inclusive, for example for children and young people with different cognitive development, literacy skills, backgrounds, family circumstances, life experiences and access needs. Moreover, methods benefit from being adaptable and imaginative. Timing and location of fieldwork are also vital to inclusivity.

As discussed in Chapter Three, involving children and young people in the research design and process has benefits both for research and the children and young people involved, and is likely to lead to policies and services that better reflect children's and young people's priorities and concerns. Of course there are challenges, not least in ensuring adequate time and resources, finding ways to engage and retain diverse children and young people in a project, and dealing with the unexpected. Every project involves new challenges and new learning, for researchers as much if not more than the children and young people. Being flexible and open to new ideas and perspectives is absolutely key, as is valuing all experience equally.

It is essential to be honest with children and young people from the outset about the scope and limitations for their involvement. Although potentially ideal, often it is not possible to do full co-production or include them at every stage, for example because of their availability and interest, resources and timing. We have found that this is rarely a problem as long as this is made clear early on. The experience and skills learnt can also be collateral benefits. Issues are more likely to arise when well-intentioned and enthusiastic researchers promise more than they can deliver, underplay how long the project will take, or overplay the potential impact and benefits, for example on service delivery. So our top tips for involving young people are to be honest, be open and have fun! In the rather dry world of research and evaluation, working alongside children and young people is hugely enjoyable as well as a great learning opportunity for all involved.

Bibliography

This book is intended as a practical guide for researchers, evaluators, research users, commissioners and others and drew on the extensive literature in this area as well as our own experience in the field. References cited are given at the end of each chapter, but there is always more to learn. This book therefore concludes with a bibliography of key references and resources, providing an overview of the wider literature.

Research with children and young people: general

Bennett, A., Cieslik, M. and Miles, S. (eds) (2003) *Researching Youth*. Basingstoke: Palgrave Macmillan.

Christensen, P. and James, A. (eds) (2008) *Research with Children: Perspectives and Practices*, 2nd edn. London: Routledge.

Clark, A., Flewitt, R., Hammersley, M. and Robb, M. (eds) (2014) *Understanding Research with Children and Young People*. London: Sage.

Goodman, G. and Worlet, N. (eds) (2014) *The Sage Handbook of Child Research*. London: Sage.

Grieg, A., Taylor, J. and Mackay, T. (2013) *Doing Research with Children: A Practical Guide*. London: Sage.

Lefevre, M. (2018) *Communicating and Engaging with Children and Young People: Making a Difference.* Bristol: Policy Press.

Lewis, A. and Lindsay, G. (2000) *Researching Children's Perspectives*. Buckingham: Open University Press.

Montgomery, H. and Robb, M. (2018) *Children and Young People's Worlds*. Bristol: Policy Press.

O'Reilly M., Ronzoni, P. and Dogra, N. (2013) *Research with Children: Theory and Practice*. London: Sage.

Qvortrup, J., Corsaro, W.A. and Honig, M.S. (2009) *The Palgrave Handbook of Childhood Studies*. Basingstoke: Palgrave Macmillan.

Shaw, C., Brady, L.M. and Davey, C. (2011) *Guidelines for Research with Children and Young People*. London: National Children's Bureau. Available from: www.ncb.org.uk/resources-publications/resources/guidelines-research-children-and-young-people

Smith, C. and Greene, S. (2014) *Key Thinkers in Childhood Studies*. Bristol: Policy Press.

Tisdall, K., Davis, J. and Gallagher, M. (2009) *Researching with Children and Young People*. London: Sage.

Journals

Childhood: a global journal of child research. http://journals.sagepub.com/home/chd

Children & Society. https://onlinelibrary.wiley.com/journal/10990860

International Journal of Child, Youth and Family Studies: www.youthpolicy.org/journals/international-journal-of-child-youth-and-family-studies/

International Journal of Children's Rights. http://booksandjournals.brillonline.com/content/journals/15718182

Involvement

Aldridge, J. (2016) *Participatory Research: Working with Vulnerable Groups in Research and Practice*. Bristol: Policy Press.

Brady, L.M., Davey, C., Shaw, C. and Blades, R. (2012) Involving children and young people in research: principles into practice. In Beresford, P. and Carr, S. (eds) *Social Care, Service Users and User Involvement: Building on Research*. London: Jessica Kingsley.

Dynamix and Save the Children (2002) *Participation: Spice it Up*. Swansea: Save the Children.

Fleming, J. and Boeck, T. (eds) (2012) *Involving Children and Young People in Health and Social Care Research*. London: Routledge.

Franks, M. (2011) Pockets of Participation: Revisiting Child-centred Participation Research. *Children & Society*, 25(1): 15–25.

Groundwater-Smith, S., Dockett, S. and Bottrell, D. (2015) *Participatory Research with Children and Young People*, London: Sage.

INVOLVE (2016) *Involving Children and Young People in Research: Top Tips for Researchers.* Southampton: INVOLVE. Available from: www. invo.org.uk/posttypenews/involving-children-and-young-people-in-research-top-tips-and-key-issues/

Kellet, M. (2005) *How to Develop Children as Researchers: A Step by Step Guide to Teaching the Research Process.* London: Sage.

McCabe, A. and Horsley, K. (2008) *The Evaluator's Cookbook: Exercises for Participatory Evaluation with Children and Young People.* London: Routledge

PEAR (2011) *Young People in Research: How to involve us. Guidance for Researchers from the PEAR Young People's Public Health Group.* London: NCB. Available from: www.ncb.org.uk/resources-publications/resources/young-people-research-guidance-researchers-pear-young-peoples

Tisdall, E.K.M., Davis, J.M., Hill, M. and Prout, A. (eds) (2006) *Children, Young People and Social Inclusion: Participation for What?* Bristol: Policy Press.

Online resources

GenerationR: young people's advisory groups for clinical research: http://generationr.org.uk/

National Children's Bureau young researchers: www.ncb.org.uk/what-we-do/what-we-do/involving-children-and-young-people/involving-children-young-people-research

NIHR INVOLVE. Information, resources and links on involving children and young people in health, public health and social care research: www.invo.org.uk/find-out-more/involving-children-and-young-people/

Open University Children's Research Centre: www.open.ac.uk/
researchprojects/childrens-research-centre/

Ethics

Alderson, P. and Morrow, V. (2011) *The Ethics of Research with Children
and Young People: A Practical Handbook*. London: Sage.

Farrell, A. (2005) *Ethical Research with Children*. Maidenhead: Open
University Press.

Graham, J., Grewal, I. and Lewis, J. (2007) *Ethics in Social Research:
The Views of Research Participants*. London, Government Social
Research. Available from: www.gov.uk/government/uploads/
system/uploads/attachment_data/file/497221/ethics_participants_
tcm6-5783.pdf

Harcourt, D., Perry, B. and Waller, T. (eds) (2011) *Researching Young
Children's Perspectives: Debating the Ethics and Dilemmas of Educational
Research with Children*. Abingdon, Oxon: Routledge.

Information Commissioners Office (2018) *Guide to the General Data
Protection Regulation for Organisations*. London: ICO. Available from:
https://ico.org.uk/for-organisations/guide-to-the-general-data-
protection-regulation-gdpr/

Information Commissioners Office (2018) *Children: Specific Data
Protection Guidance in Relation to Research with Children and Young
People*. London: ICO. Available from: https://ico.org.uk/for-
organisations/guide-to-the-general-data-protection-regulation-
gdpr/applications/children/

Iphofen, R. (2011) *Ethical Decision-making in Social Research: A Practical
Guide*. London: Macmillan.

Iphofen, R. (2017) *Finding Common Ground: Consensus in Research
Ethics Across the Social Sciences*. Advances in Research Ethics and
Integrity, vol. 1. Bingley, UK: Emerald Publishing.

Israel, M. and Hay, I. (2006) *Research Ethics for Social Scientists*. London:
Sage.

Richards, S., Clark, J. and Boggis, A. (2015) *Ethical Research with
Children: Untold Narratives and Taboos*. Basingstoke: Palgrave
Macmillan.

Sheffield University (2012) *Specialist Research Ethics Guidance Paper-Research involving adult participants who lack the capacity to consent.* Sheffield: Sheffield University. Available from: www.sheffield.ac.uk/polopoly_fs/1.165638!/file/SREGP-Adults-LCC.pdf

Online resources

Association of Internet Researchers, ethical and social media research. https://aoir.org/ethics

Economic and Social Research Council (ESRC) (2005) *Research Ethics Framework.* Available from: https://esrc.ukri.org/funding/guidance-for-applicants/research-ethics/

ERIC: International Ethical Research Involving Children project. http://childethics.com/

ESRC *The Research Ethics Guidebook: A Resource for Social Researchers.* Available from: www.ethicsguidebook.ac.uk/Confidentiality-73

ESRC guidance on online research: www.ethicsguidebook.ac.uk/Online-research-102

ESRC guidance on mental capacity and consent: MC Act and Adults with incapacity http://ethicsguidebook.ac.uk/Consent-72; http://ethicsguidebook.ac.uk/Legal-requirements-76; https://esrc.ukri.org/funding/guidance-for-applicants/research-ethics/frequently-raised-questions/what-is-freely-given-informed-consent/

Health Research Authority (2017) *Applying a Proportionate Approach to the Process of Seeking Consent: HRA Guidance.* London: HRA. Available from: www.hra.nhs.uk/planning-and-improving-research/best-practice/informing-participants-and-seeking-consent/

Health Research Authority (2018) *Consent and Participant Information Sheet Preparation Guidance.* London: HRA. www.hra-decisiontools.org.uk/consent/

Jones, C. (2011) Ethical issues in online research, British Educational Research Association online resource. www.bera.ac.uk/researchers-resources/publications/ethical-issues-in-online-research

Market Research Society (MRS) (2018) *Data Protection Research: Guidance for MRS Members and Company Partners, 2018*. London: Market Research Society. Available from: www.mrs.org.uk/pdf/MRS%20Data%20Protection%20and%20Research%20Guidance%20Section%201%20_28.04.2018.pdf

Mental Capacity Act 2005 England; Adults with Incapacity (Scotland) Act 2000

NHS guidance: Mental Capacity Act: www.nhs.uk/Conditions/social-care-and-support-guide/Pages/mental-capacity.aspx) and www.shef.ac.uk/polopoly_fs/1.165638!/file/SREGP-Adults-LCC.pdf

Social Research Association (2019) *Ethics Guidelines*. London: SRA. http://the-sra.org.uk/research-ethics/ethics-guidelines/

UK Evaluation Society. *Good Practice Guidance*. www.evaluation.org.uk/about-us/publications

Methods

'Creative Methods with Young People' (2012) Special issue, *International Journal of Social Research Methodology*, 15(2). Available from: www.tandfonline.com/toc/tsrm20/15/2

Foster, V. (2015) *Collaborative Arts-based Research for Social Justice*. London: Routledge.

Green, S. and Hogan, D. (2005) *Researching Children's Experience: Approaches and Methods*. London: Sage.

Kara, H. (2015) *Creative Research Methods in the Social Sciences: A Practical Guide,* London: Policy Press.

Stuart, K., Maynard, L. and Rouncefield, C. (2015) *Evaluation Practice for Projects with Young People: A Guide to Creative Research*. London: Sage.

Smee, H. (2008) *Web 2.0 as a Social Sciences Research Tool*. London: British Library. Available from: www.bl.uk/reshelp/bldept/socsci/socint/web2/web2.pdf

Veale, A. (2005) Creative methodologies in participatory research with children. In Greene, S. and Hogan, D. (eds) *Researching Children's Experience: Approaches and Methods*. London: Sage.

Williams, L. (2009) *Young children's Voices Network; Listening as a Way of Life*. London: NCB. Available from: www.ncb.org.uk/listening-and-participation-resources

Online resources

ICC/ESOMAR International Codes on Market, Opinion and Social Research and Data Analytics, including guidelines on research with children and young people and using social media. www.esomar.org/what-we-do/code-guidelines

ESRC/NatCen project: 'New social media, new social science?' http://nsmnss.blogspot.co.uk/

Young Digital: web resource on digital research with children and young people. www.youngdigital.net

Index

Page numbers is *italics* indicate figures and tables.

Series editors:

Patten Smith, Ipsos MORI Research Methods Centre

Ivana La Valle, University of East London & independent consultant

The SRA Shorts Series is a research methods series in the Policy Press Shorts format. They provide research practitioners, academics and research users with short, high-quality and focused guides to specific topics within the field of social research methods.

The series provides a voice for social research and practical guidance for researchers to improve research quality. It focuses on social research and practice, offering the chance to highlight the impact of research on practice and policy and to draw attention to new and innovative research methods.

Features of the series:

*   Books will be between 20 - 50,000 words long, equivalent to 50 - 150 pages.
*   The content will be practical and accessible.
*   Books will be of interest to an international audience.

Available now:

Demystifying evaluation by David Parsons, Feb 2017